Midlife Moon

From Darkness to Bright Light

A novel by,

Sameer Zahr

(Love Is All There Is) Book 7

Midlife Moon
Copyright © 2021 by Sameer Zahr

All rights reserved. No part of this publication may be reproduced, distributed, or transmitted in any form or by any means, including photocopying, recording, or other electronic or mechanical methods, without the prior written permission of the author, except in the case of brief quotations embodied in critical reviews and certain other non-commercial uses permitted by copyright law.

ISBN
978-1-954168-85-5 (Hardcover)
978-1-954168-84-8 (Paperback)
978-1-954168-83-1 (eBook)

Table of Contents

Prologue vii
Chapter 1　Good Buddies, But Different 1
Chapter 2　Seeking Guidance 9
Chapter 3　The Ugly and the Beautiful 18
Chapter 4　Hope Vs. Despair 29
Chapter 5　New Threats and Demands 41
Chapter 6　Court Hearings and New Surprises 55
Chapter 7　Court Orders and a New Beginning 66
Chapter 8　A Legal Blowout 78
Chapter 9　Commitment to Change 88
Chapter 10　A Definite Awakening 100
Chapter 11　A Brighter Side Of The Moon 110
Chapter 12　Continued Affirmations 122
Chapter 13　A new Adventure 135
Chapter 14　The Challenge Ahead 145
Chapter 15　A Brighter Moonlight 162
Chapter 16　The Sun Takes Over From the Moon 176
Epilogue 191

Prologue

I was awakened by a hard knock on the door. It was 2:00 am on a cold Saturday morning in New York City. I put my robe on and rushed to find out who is there at such an odd hour. I looked through the peephole and I saw the troubled face of my friend, Freddie. I quickly opened the door and had to hold him from falling on the ground. He was evidently wasted drunk, and found it convenient to come to me. I helped him to sit on the sofa, and neither one of us said a word.

He looked at me with his bleary and watery red eyes and stuttered few words I could not understand. He continued to mutter and blabber, repeating himself with wide sweeping gestures of his hands and arms while leaning forward to get my attention. I interrupted him and said,

"Sit back Freddie, let me make you some coffee now."

"Oookay… Barry… thanks… !"

Three minutes later I came back with the coffee and found him asleep on the sofa, snoring loud. I decided not to wake him up. I took off his coat, jacket and shoes, loosened his necktie and stretched him on the sofa. I put a pillow under his head and covered him with a thick blanket to keep him warm. I went back to sleep in my bedroom and wondered about my close friend Freddie. His life had recently gone upside down since he decided to leave his wife Matilda and their two lovely boys. This was not the first time Freddie sought shelter in my place drunk and confused. My place was closer to his drinking hole, than the hotel suite he was staying at.

I got up at 7:00 am, though it was not a working day. I remembered that Freddie was sleeping on the sofa outside. I checked on him and he was still asleep on his back, breathing and snoring with his jaws opened to help him breathe. I went straight to the kitchen and made a fresh pot of coffee and toasted two slices of bread to serve with butter and jam. As soon as I walked out of the kitchen, I saw Freddie turning, and he slowly opened his eyes. He looked at me and saw me carrying the tray in my hands. He smiled and said,

"Oh Coffee! Yummy… and toast… what a service!"

"Okay, you trouble maker, sit up… and enjoy this last service from me."

"I love visiting with you… you spoil me!" Freddie said.

"Don't get used to it dear fellow… you have to finally grow up and straighten your act. Don't abuse our friendship with… your drunkard behavior. So, drink coffee, eat and tell me what happened… the reason which created this honorable and pleasant visit to my place!" I said, while watching him devour the toast and sipping big gulps of coffee. A minute later Freddie sat up and asked if I had pills to ease his hangover headache.

"At your service my lord! Now tell me what happened?"

"Umm… I had a fight." Freddie said and went silent.

"With whom, your ex, Matilda or… your new flame, Jane?"

"Yup… that one."

"Why?" I asked.

"The usual… she wants more money, and marriage." Freddie said.

"And…?" I asked.

"What and? I will not do it I—I am not officially divorced yet, and it's been less than a year with Jane… I am tired of this relationship already. I want to quit. I'm 43 and so confused… though I hate to live alone…

"Before I forget, I also had an interesting dream last night… I was lying down on my back in a vast grass field, looking up quietly at the stars and the midnight sky… A full moon suddenly appeared. It was yellowish in color and big—I mean *BIG*.

"I kept focusing on it, and it me frustrated me. I got upset and mad when the clouds covered its face. I waited for a while, then the clouds moved away, and that cheered up tremendously. I saw the moon shine brightly on my face… and I—I saw myself smiling and happy for a couple of minutes. Then the moon's face was covered again with clouds. That made me upset again. These shifts from dark to—to bright kept repeating themselves for several minutes… and along with it I was shifting from feelings of sadness to feelings of joy… Then suddenly I woke up! Um… What do you make of it Barry?"

"I can't tell exactly... It could be a confirmation that you're going through your midlife crisis? What you described you saw are signs of instability in your life. They reflect on what you're going through nowadays... Do you agree?" I said facetiously.

"Yea right! You're a great help to me... You can't find anything good to say about me? Thanks, anyhow!"

CHAPTER 1

Good Buddies, But Different

Freddie Rodman and I, Barry Green, were college buddies. We both graduated with our MBA degrees from Columbia University in New York. I later worked as a stockbroker on Wall Street, and recently promoted to an investment director position. Freddie chose to be in the real estate business, which his father had started. He succeeded to build it up into a small empire. He owned various apartment and commercial buildings in New York, and in few other cities around the country. He ran his operations from an office in Manhattan, and had a good-sized staff to help him manage the business.

Freddie and I have been best friends for more than twenty years. We used to hang out with other boys and girls in college and we had a lot of fun. Freddie was very popular among the women due to his good looks and sense of humor. He's 6ft1in tall with auburn hair, wide shoulders and an athletic slim body. His masculine face, with his beautiful green eyes, sharp nose and full lips helped him to attract many beautiful girls at that time.

I, on the other hand, was not as tall, about 5ft10 in slightly overweight but otherwise, good-looking. I have blue eyes, blondish color hair, dainty nose and thin lips. The girls liked me for my jovial personality and my spontaneous jokes that made them laugh.

Freddie came from a more privileged background and his father authorized him to expand their real estate business before he passed away. I, however, had no help and succeeded to adapt to Wall Street stressful conditions and high standards all on my own.

Both Freddie and I got married around the same time. We were both 28 years old and we married women we met at the University. I got divorced three years ago, and as we did not have children, the separation was amicable and mutual. I've been living alone ever since, except for occasional short relationships, and I was cool about it. Freddie was not happily married and left his wife seven months ago with two teenage boys. His guilt feelings increased over leaving the children behind.

He started a new relationship with Jane Neiman, which was not based on love. He was attracted to her passionate and seductive appeal. She was of average height but blessed with a well-shaped and sexy body. She had brown eyes and brown hair crowning her white face and dainty nose over her luscious lips.

Jane showed no interest in developing a relationship with Freddie's children, and that created a lot of friction between them. She did not even care to diminish his guilt feelings with genuine love. She was mainly interested to satisfy her own material and financial needs. Matilda, his wife on the other hand, was a good woman and a good mother. She's a beautiful woman, well educated and well mannered. She was 5ft.8in tall, and she carried herself well despite a few extra pounds added after her two pregnancies. Her piercing blue eyes and sharp nose helped define her strong character.

She loved Freddie and was heart-broken when she found out he was sleeping around. That prompted the divorce action on her part, which continued to be ugly and far from being settled. He was allowed to see the boys every other weekend but was not on speaking terms with Matilda. The lawyers on both sides were still fighting it out and that was a very stressful experience for Freddie.

Freddie and I discussed his divorce on various occasions. We tried to figure out how to simplify its complications, but at the end the lawyers ruled. As expected, Matilda's lawyers wanted 50% of his net assets, while his lawyers were holding back at 25%, including the high value of the family house in Westchester county New York. He rented a suite at a hotel in Midtown Manhattan on a monthly basis. Some nights he stayed with Jane, if they did not have a fight. Freddie followed his heart's desire for passion and Jane succeeded to satisfy his needs, provided he took good care of her with a hefty sum every month.

***

Slowly thereafter, Freddie started drinking heavily and more frequently. He just wanted to escape from his responsibility to face reality. He was living in denial. His ego wouldn't allow him to reconcile with his wife, and Jane took advantage of his weakness in bed and did her best to benefit from it materially. So, when Freddie came to my place drunk that night I fully understood that he was seeking help. I wanted to tell him that he needs to see a psychiatrist that same morning at my place, but I chickened out. Instead, I asked him,

"So what do you think you should do now Freddie?"

"I have to end my relationship with Jane, and live alone for a while. I need to find out um… what I really want from my life. I will try to establish direct communication with Matilda and ask if I could see the children more often." Freddie expressed affirmatively.

"Now you're talking, that's a positive attitude. Do it and don't hesitate. You need to get out of the misery you put yourself into. Breaking up with Jane should be easy she cannot sue you for alimony, as you did not live together. Re-establishing contact with your Matilda may be difficult but doable. I know her, um… she can be reasonable though, a stubborn woman. You may have to apologize to her first and confess you hurt her. Tell her you broke up with Jane. You have nothing to fear Get it off your chest and hope for the best." I said, to encourage him to do it.

"Listen, thank you for sheltering me last night, you are truly my best friend and I'll keep you posted on what develops."

***

Freddie went to his hotel. He showered and changed his clothes. He called Jane and told her they need to talk and that he's coming over to see her.

Jane was nervous and thought it had to do with the argument they had the night before. She smiled at him, still wearing her sexy lingerie when he walked in, but that did not weaken Freddie from doing what he went there for. He sat down at a chair distant from where she was sitting and said,

"Jane, I came here um to tell you that I—I can't see you anymore."

Jane was silent for a minute, wiped the smile off her face, covered her exposed legs and simply asked,

"Why?"

"It has nothing to do with you… you are a good woman and I am sorry if I vented out some of my frustrations on you. I have a lot of issues to sort out and um… I need to do it alone, on my own."

"So you want a break up with me?" Jane responded with a question.

"Yes, I do! I want a break away from any one or anything that might derail me from my desired focus on me. I don't know who I am anymore. I don't know me, and I continue to dwell on my past and it's killing me. I have to do a lot of soul-searching, please understand!" Freddie explained compassionately.

"Uh, you don't think I can help you?"

"No, I don't think anyone can help me, even a psychoanalyst. I have to figure out how I can help myself", Freddie said.

"So what do you plan to do now?" Jane curiously asked.

"Other than being alone, I don't have um… any specific plans. I need to think hard and thorough. I will consult with the Divine Power to guide me." Freddie said.

"Well… there's nothing I can do then? Are you going to give me money to continue to live comfortably?" Jane asked.

"I gave you a lot already, why do you need more?"

"You broke my heart and suddenly you want to disappear! How am I going to keep the living standard you spoiled me with? Did you think you could just turn your back and walk away so easily?" Jane said sarcastically.

"Sorry it's not working well between us, it's best we part as friends. We argue and fight a lot, it's not healthy for either one of us."

"Okay fine, if you want to leave me go ahead! But bear in mind you owe me… and I expect you to honor your end of the deal." Jane demanded.

"What deal?" Freddie asked.

"I waited for you to get divorced and marry me, wasn't that we discussed and what I wanted?" Jane explained facetiously.

"Yeah! That's what *you* wanted. I—I never promised you anything." Freddie insisted.

"Okay, you can go now! But I expect you to give me a hefty monthly check as you used to, for the next three years, until I find someone else to take care of me, if I'm lucky!"

"Don't count on anything, and goodbye!" Freddie said, stood up and walked away.

Freddie felt relieved and not afraid of her threats. A big block of cement was lifted off his back. He went to the hotel to rest for a short while before calling Matilda. Half an hour later he called her,

"Hi Matilda, Freddie here, can we talk?"

"Talk about what?"

"About us having a civil relationship. It is not to discuss the legal case. For the sake of our long years together, I would like to tell you what's happening in my life, perhaps we can reconcile our differences and perhaps um.. start communicating again!" Freddie gently interceded. Matilda went silent for few seconds then said,

"What? You now regret the damage you caused, and all of a sudden you want to fix it?"

"Yeah, why not?" Freddie Asked.

"Uh huh! Sorry sir, the jar is broken and shattered to pieces, and it cannot be fixed. So?" Matilda said angrily.

"Would you think about it, at least for the boys' sake?" Freddie begged.

"Forget about it, I've already moved on in my life, go find out who you are… and what you want from your life, and good luck!" Matilda said angrily and hung up.

The conversation was short and Freddie was devastated by her bitter attitude and lack of willingness to forgive him. Maybe she met someone else, he thought? He didn't want to bother me again, the good old me, his shadow and his only shoulder to cry on. He had quite an eventful morning and decided to take a long walk in Central Park and mull over the turmoil in his life.

***

He walked on until he reached the back of the Metropolitan museum 30 minutes later. He sat on a bench and wished he had a notebook to write down his fresh thoughts. Instead, he took out his smartphone from his pocket and started typing down in his 'notes' application. He wrote,

> *I am 43 years old and alone, without my family. After 15 years of a decent married life with two children, I have no one to hug now. I allowed my illusion of a passionate relationship to convince me that I deserve someone better than my wife. I*

*was blinded by my thoughts that passion would be the answer to my 'unfulfilled' satisfaction at home. I was wrong. My initial expectation that my relationship with Jane would do the job was an illusion, totally unfounded. It turned out to be a proof of my total ignorance about what **true love** is all about.*

I am not a happy person now. I built a decent business and lived comfortably and provided more than what my family needed. Success did not make me really happy. On the contrary, it boosted my ego and developed within me a false feeling that I was invincible.

Every time I spent with my children I sensed their anger against me, and that reignited the guilt feelings within. Brian, is 13 and Mark, is 11. And I am not there when they need me the most at such a tender age.

The current circumstances are terrible. I escape and hide behind my excessive drinking during my free weekends. I am losing my friends one after the other. I only have my loyal buddy, Barry. My extended family does not care about what is going on in my life either. I tried few sessions with a psychotherapist but that did not help. I am now at a loss of what I should do to bring back some joy into my life. I feel empty inside. I've become a body without a soul. I am suffering from despair, and I'm trying my best not to make stupid decisions.

Apart form my non-existent social life, I am not as focused at work as I used to be. I seem to delegate too much authority to my two managers who occasionally made bad decisions. The early excitement for hard work and success has slowly disappeared, and I didn't care. My father passed away few years ago and my mother is pre-occupied with her social engagements. I have no brothers or sisters to help me in my business. I stopped working out, and I don't take care of my health, as if I enjoy punishing myself. I am at a very low point in my life and can't figure out how to climb out of the dark hole I fell in.

I can only pray for divine guidance now, and leave it to the Universe to show me what to do next.

Freddie finished his writing and put his mobile device back in his inside pocket. He wanted to rest for few minutes to reflect on his current state of being. He looked around and he saw two Buddhist monks sitting on the bench next to him, eating some dried fruits and nuts from a plastic bag, and laughing joyously. It was evident they were very happy. Their unexpected presence next to Freddie was not a coincidence. He took it as a sign from the divine Universe he just wrote about. He courageously went to go talk to them, and find out their secret for happiness.

"Hello, I am sorry to interrupt you, can I ask you a question?" Freddie politely asked the two monks.

They looked at one another with a gracious smile then looked back at him and one of them answered in his noticeable foreign accent, and said,

"No problem… how can we help you?"

"Thank you, I noticed how happy you are and I would like to know what's your secret?"

"Hum, short question… but long answer!" The monk said in his broken English.

"Please try in few words, I know you can!" Freddie insisted.

"First find out who you are, then ask yourself 'what do I really want'… then surrender to Universe. It will guide you."

"Is that a long process?" Freddie asked.

"Depends how big you desire change, maybe weeks, months or years… how hungry are you to know?" The monk said with a smile.

"What brings you to New York, if I may ask?"

"Invited by Buddhist temple in city… branch our organization… we give lectures tonight… you come?"

"I'll be happy to, tell me where!" Freddie said.

The monk gave him a card with the address and the name of the organization. He understood their broken English and thanked them. He said he will see them later.

Freddie looked at the card and it was an invitation to a silent retreat at the Garrison Institute, one hour north of Manhattan, located on the banks of the Hudson River. It was a retreat based on the Buddhist teachings on behalf of a temple in New York City. The monks told him that the next day Sunday is a special welcome to beginners who are seeking peace and tranquility in their lives. There will be lectures followed by meditations.

Freddie called Barry and asked if he could see him briefly that afternoon. He wanted to discuss the idea of going to the retreat with him. Barry welcomed him, and they agreed to meet around 3 pm the same Saturday afternoon.

Freddie arrived on time and I asked him when he sat down looking excited about something,

"What are you so excited about? Wow, I'm so lucky you want to see me again… twice the same day?"

"Okay, Hear me for a second. First, I want to tell you that I broke up with Jane, and then I tried to re-connect with Matilda but she refused to talk, or to see me. So, I went for a walk in the Park and um… I met two Buddhist monks who gave me this card, when I asked them what was the secret for their happiness. They invited me to go tomorrow to this retreat upstate, would you like to join me?" Freddie answered me with a question.

"First, I'm happy you broke up with Jane, and I'm sorry to hear that Matilda 'shut the door' in your face. I know how it feels to be rejected. It is good that you are considering to find peace and happiness again, and this retreat is a good start… but sorry I can't join you I have other plans." I said.

"Fine then, I'll go alone. I'll drive. It should be a relaxing short trip. I need to open up to such possibilities that can help me get out of my misery." Freddie said.

"Good! Go and find out. Call me when you're back!"

***

When Freddie left, I started wondering again about the troublesome gyrations that have been going on in his life since his divorce. He had such great success building up a good business and we used to have so much fun together. He had a stable life at home and at work. He's different now. He is seeking guidance from Eastern cultures and spiritual practices? I sense that he is giving up on his current state of affairs. I am somewhat worried about him and I hope he'll stabilize soon!

CHAPTER 2

Seeking Guidance

Freddie woke up very early on Sunday, got dressed casually and drove north to the Garrison Institute. He arrived at 8:00 am, which was already late as they had started the day at 6:00 am with meditation and breakfast. Freddie was spotted by one of the monks he met in the Park. He came to him and offered him a seat in the big room where a lecture was about to start. There were more than 100 people in the room. The keynote speaker was one of the senior Lamas, who works closely with the Dalai Lama in Dharamsala, India, the headquarters of the Tibetan Government in exile.

The Lama spoke very good English and the title of his speech was "Who Am I?". I took notes of some main points,

> *"Another way of understanding this question is to call it Self Inquiry, or the Awakening Event. You start by observing your sensations, impulses, feelings, thoughts and consciousness. You try to find a soul or a self in the process of searching, and you realize such a thing does not exist. Why? Because we are connected to all that is, not just our selves.*
>
> *"The purpose behind the practice of self-inquiry is to achieve self-realization. The first thing to trigger the process is to minimize your physical and external distractions. Then you need to have a sincere desire to know who you really are. Learn how to simply relax your mind to be quiet. Your mind will start to do numbers on you and start rationalizing. This creates resistance and it block inner search to connect with the divine or higher self. Focus on your sincere intention to*

know who you are and repeat asking yourself the question "Who Am I?".

"Be as open in your mind as possible. Surrender to the truth even though you don't know what it is yet and become an open receptacle. You will experience mental blocks and insights racing through your mind.

"Do not begin the process of self-realization with any pre-conceived ideas of who you are. Despite the inspiration you may get from spiritual teachers, do not continue with the process with their teachings in mind. This unique discovery is just between you and Truth itself.

"The destination of your journey is to arrive at the Truth. Once you get there, you achieve self-realization. You will discover that the self is you, a changeless and a state of complete consciousness. You are not your body or any of your senses, or even your mind, you are simply a conscious being. You are always present and above all physical senses. You are not separate from the rest of the Universe."

The Lama spoke for about one hour and the above remarks were all I could note down. What was very important in his speech was that this process of finding out "Who Am I", is not an overnight process. It is long-term practice that could take months or years to master.

There was a 20-minute tea or coffee break before the second lecture. I noticed how happy people were during the break. They all seemed to be good students of the spiritual realm. I just roamed around with a cup of coffee and listened to the insightful conversations some of these people had.

A Buddhist monk from San Francisco gave the second lecture. He was introduced as an American scholar who is a master of meditation. His message was "Meditation and Self-Love". Again I tried my best to take as many notes as possible. I jotted down the following:

"We live an over-whelming life loaded with confusion and distractions. We work hard to make money, have a family and live a good life. Then we find ourselves over-charged or

burned out. We forget about self-love and how to regroup with our sacred self.

"To learn how to love our selves we need to learn how to meditate. It connects us with our true self. It teaches us presence and how to experience inner calm.

"We will try meditation together before the end of this session. It is a simple process that helps us to change our state of being. Meditation teaches us how to forgive, to understand and how to solve personal problems. There are no set rules, just try to be still and be present kicking all past memories out of your mind.

"We learn how to connect with the Higher Self, the infinite field of all potentialities. That field is also called the 'Love Intelligence'. We start feeling Love around us and particularly inwardly within us. We start loving our selves and knowing that we are worthy beings. We feel we are rich inside us and we learn how to bridge this wealth outside us as well. Meditation is truly a healing process that cleanses the soul. It is Love in action. It is a true path to happiness..."

Freddie felt a new stream of thoughts racing in his head while listening to him:

"I felt he was directly talking to him. The monk then started the process of meditation for 15 minutes. He instructed everyone how to sit straight, close our eyes, breathe and relax then allowed us to practice it. The whole room turned quiet and it was the first time I meditate, ever. The first half of my meditation was a battle of mental races with all kinds of thoughts that kept my focus elsewhere. After remembering what the teacher said, I began to kick out these interfering thoughts, and felt a sudden calm within me for a short while. That gave me a glimpse of how to quiet my mind, and I sensed some inner appreciation of 'who I am'. It made me taste a bit of what self-love is all about."

A minute later a soft bell rang and we stopped and opened our eyes. The monk asked how many of us experienced a connection with the Higher Self or Love Intelligence. Almost 60% of the people in the room raised their hands. He told us, the ones who really didn't experience the connection, not to be discouraged and with practice it will be achieved.

The plan was to have lunch as a last event of the retreat. Freddie decided not to stay for lunch and he drove back to the City with a new head on his shoulders, grateful to have made the decision to attend these two lectures. It was an eye-opening experience. He was angry why he did not search for such communities before, and he decided to do what's necessary to change the course of his life.

***

He couldn't stop thinking about the half day he just had. It was as if there was another world out there and he had no idea what it was like. His mind was racing with ideas about what to do next. He decided to take it easy the rest of the day and to just reflect on what he went through and review the notes he took.

Freddie sat down and reviewed his lecture notes. From the first lecture he surmised that self-realization would not be attained overnight. Similarly, meditation requires perseverance and many repetitions before it is mastered. He thought to himself:

> *"I know there are Buddhist temples and meditation centers here in the City, would that be adequate to try out first? Otherwise, I would have to go on a sabbatical to India or Tibet, to find out 'who I am' and learn how to 'meditate', in an ashram or monastery. Perhaps a change of environment and scenery would be timely. How about seeing the kids if I leave for a long while? What should my priority be, concerned about others or take care of my miserable state of being?"*

Freddie couldn't make up his mind and decided to sleep on it. He tossed and turned and had an unsettling night. He asked for guidance and his subconscious mind kept pushing him to his past experiences. He had confusing dreams of him walking lost in busy streets and contrasted with scenes of quiet surroundings in snow-capped mountains. He tried to interpret his dreams and all that he could think of was his busy life in Manhattan vs. his quiet life in the mountains. He had a conscious decision to make, what will he choose?

He spent his day at the office and tried hard to concentrate on the work at hand. His mind continued to race with the images of his dream. He felt he was imprisoned by his misery and desperately looking for the exit out the prison. He briefly tasted the meaningful benefit of meditation and that assured him that it would the right practice to follow. His main quest was to find the answers to *'Who Am I'* and *'What Do I Want?'* from my life. Why am I here, and what is my life purpose?

Freddie needed to talk to someone he trusted as a sounding board, and the only one he could think of is me, his 'alter ego'. He called me, who else, and asked if we could have dinner together to talk about important matters. I agreed. We met and Freddie started,

"Thank you for coming. I listened to two lectures on Sunday. One was about self-realization, as an answer to the question 'Who Am I', and the other was about the benefits of meditation. That experience shook me up. I realized that I would slowly destroy myself, if I don't change my current condition. I want to pursue this search… the question is whether I look for it while staying here in the city… or go somewhere far, like India. What do you think?"

"Hum… you're still carrying great guilt within you, huh? One thing I know is that pursuing these practices of inner search is by far better than escaping to get drunk. It's interesting how the western cultures and religions could not be as appealing to the process of inner healing, as the Eastern Cultures. You know, there are many temples and meditation centers here in the City, I suggest you try that out first um… before you go far." I said.

"I don't know? And by the way, you got divorced too… how come you are enjoying a better life than me?" Freddie enviously asked me.

"First, we didn't have children and, you and I are different, I did not cheat on my ex as you did. We broke up because we out-grew our relationship. We both changed and decided to breakup in a friendly way. That's why I don't have any guilt feelings… you smart elk." I responded with piercing eyes.

"Okay fine, you said enough… I'm just jealous. But, how come you didn't have another long relationship since your 'friendly' divorce?" Freddie asked sarcastically.

"I am not interested! I enjoy being busy at work and see my friends on occasion, besides I have to first meet the woman that I can connect with. I am also your age remember? The women that are available are either too young or divorced. The few short relationships I've had are more than enough for me. I am free, and I might have someone soon!" I truthfully explained.

"Don't you miss being loved by someone?" Freddie asked curiously.

"I do! I'm focused on loving my self first. The rest is secondary. I learned how to practice self-love my man… self-love." I stated emphatically.

"Do you consider yourself self-realized?"

"Self-realization, or self-actualization is when you realize your full potential. Very few can achieve that. Abraham Lincoln and Albert Einstein are supposed to have done that. I don't know if I qualify to be among this elite group of people." I said philosophically.

"So do you think um … I will be wasting my time to try and become self-realized?" Freddie asked.

"I don't know the answer, if you are not born with that gift, you may need a long time to achieve it. I don't know um… if you go to a monastery for a couple of months that it will be sufficient to do the job. You may need years of practice. I believe it is best you try it out here first, you will know better after few months of schooling and meditating… I don't know!"

"On another subject, Barry, do you think Jane will contact me again?" Freddie asked.

"Why are you asking? Do you miss being with her already? Are you sick in your head? Do you um… like to suffer again? If so, go ahead and call her! But if you do, please find another shoulder to lean on."

"Oh come on Barry! What if she sues me for leaving her?" Freddie explained.

"Okay, if you want to live in fear, go ahead and enjoy it… why would she sue you? Did you move in with her? No, so relax and focus on your life, learn how to meditate and find out who you are. Be a good example to your children, they need your attention."

"Fine Preacher! Thank you for this conversation and we'll keep in touch."

***

Freddie decided to check out the centers in Manhattan the next day and see what they offer. He found online the Self-Realization Fellowship, a worldwide organization with a well-established center located on 28th Street in Manhattan. He saw that they have regular lectures, classes and meditation sessions similar to the one he experienced at The Garrison Institute.

He called them. He was invited for an interview with the administrator in charge. He learned that the Fellowship is considered as a church to all religions. He also read that famous people like George Harrison of the Beatles, Ravi Shankar the sitar musician, and Elvis Presley were among the celebrities that were associated with the Fellowship.

Freddie had his meeting with the monk in charge and felt comfortable with the teachings program. He registered to join, and the first session to be held in three days. He also noticed they have special meditations for beginners. He was grateful to the whole new arrangement, which started with meeting the two monks in the park. He also realized that what he is doing will not be in conflict with his catholic background, as the teachings embraced all religions.

He slept better that night and the rest of the week was uneventful except for the first session at the Fellowship Friday evening, and the visit of the two boys on Saturday. He was warmly received and he shook hands with at least twenty people who welcomed him. He was overwhelmed by their love and compassion. The lecture was insightful. It emphasized the concept that we can potentially connect as 'one' with the Invisible presence of God. The meditation was more meaningful than the first one at Garrison, and he hoped it would further improve in the future.

His visit with the two boys, Brian and Mark was much easier to handle without feeling guilty to the extent he did before. During dinner he told them,

"Listen my sons, I was not very truthful to you before, when I um… told you why your mother and I broke up. It was my decision and I am solely the one to blame. I hurt her feelings because hum… I cheated on her. I broke our wedding vows … the reason why she became so upset. I don't blame her and I am sorry for breaking our unit as a family. Please forgive me! I am trying to reconcile with your mom, and hope we can be friends again. By the way, I don't have a girl friend anymore, and I am alone now. So?"

"Why did it take you so long to—to admit that, Dad?" Brian asked.

"Hum… it's my ego. I lied to myself by denying that I did something wrong. I suffered from that rationalization… and I became very guilty about what I did to you… and your mom. I'm trying hard to get rid of my guilt and it's not easy. I love you and I hope you love me back. I need you, Sons!" Freddie said, with tears falling on his cheeks. The boys got up and hugged their father and told him,

"We love you too, Dad." The rest of the weekend was spent with laughter, games, a movie and good meals together.

***

Freddie went to his office Monday morning and as soon as got out of the elevator a man served him with a subpoena. Jane was suing him for damages and claiming a hefty compensation because he left her with nothing. Freddie didn't know whether to laugh or to take it seriously. He referred the case to his lawyers and he told them on the phone,

"This is bizarre! But please fight this one out. Meanwhile, I would like to settle with my wife, Please finish the case and I don't care how much more you have to give her."

"We hear you Freddie, this Jane has no grounds to support her claims. She will lose. As to your case, we understand and will see what we can do and will get your approval before we finish with Matilda's lawyers."

Freddie wanted to lighten his load, not make it heavier. This claim by Jane was uncalled for, and he had no other choice but to defend his case.

He had met Jane at a bar about a year ago, while he was still married living at home. Jane was 27 years old and had just gotten out of a relationship, she alleged she had. Freddie didn't care about her past. He was mainly interested to have a passionate relationship with her. She figured him out and played her game. She demanded financial support in return to her willingness to please him.

She was beautiful with long legs, and looked very seductive. He escorted her to her place and spent two hours with her in bed. That was the hook that eventually led to his divorce and his misery. His wife found out and he admitted the truth. The kids couldn't understand what was going on, and walking out on them laid heavy on Freddie's mind. He took full responsibility for his own decisions, and paid his price dearly.

Freddie grew up feeling unloved by his rich parents. They were focused on other social and business attractions. His father had his business as his main interest in life, while his mother worked hard to be a socialite among her peers. Freddie had an English governess to look after him and he missed out on getting the parental love to feel secure with himself. His idea about family love and commitment was distorted. This weakness surfaced during his marriage to Matilda. She had a different upbringing and was truly loved by her parents. That made it easy for her to be loyal to her husband, and a great mother to her two boys.

Freddie's issue was his misunderstanding of what passionate love is. He thought since passion did not last long during his marriage, he then was entitled to find it elsewhere. When Matilda found out that he was cheating on her, she filed for divorce. He thought it could be reconciled and that she would forgive him. His boosted ego about himself led him to live in denial.

That careless attitude did not work, and when he moved out he started blaming the separation on Jane instead, and they argued and fought a lot. He later realized that self-denial is not the answer. The longer the separation lasted the more stubborn Matilda became, rejecting his attempts to reconcile. The lawyers had a field day with the complicated divorce case, and settlement was not in the offing. He broke up with Jane and now she was suing him.

CHAPTER 3

The Ugly and the Beautiful

I hadn't seen Freddie for more than one week, so I called him to see how he's doing. We agreed to have dinner together that evening. After we sat down I asked,

"How are you doing now? I haven't seen you in a while, which is good news somehow, as no one has woken me up after midnight lately?"

"It's been an interesting week Barry… I had a good time with my kids this past weekend… I attended my first Fellowship meeting last Friday, and I got sued by Jane!" Freddie responded.

"What? Sued by Jane? What was that about?" I curiously asked.

"It's about money, what else?"

"So, what do you intend to do about that?" I asked.

"Fight! I have no other choice. The lawyers agree that she has no grounds to stand on, and I also told them I want to finish with Matilda at any cost. I want to start on a clean slate now, I must move on!" Freddie said.

"You gave up on reconciling with Matilda?"

"Yes I did. Besides, I am not eager to get back with her anymore." Freddie said firmly.

"I see! That's new. Do you think she does not love you now?" I asked.

"It doesn't matter either way, I want to live alone now, like you. You see, I am jealous!" Freddie said with a smile.

"Yeah… yeah but of course I'll wait and see how long you will last before you hook up with another sexy woman." I responded facetiously.

"Barry, I am hoping that my Fellowship sessions will help me to control my appetite for passion, hence you don't need to worry about me and other women."

"Uh ha, I know you Freddie, better than any Fellowship or Monastery or Guru, or whatever you want to call it… It is your main weakness my man! You love to be loved by the wrong kind… you can be easily fooled into another relationship, just like the one you had with Jane. I've also seen how you—you dated when you were a student." I told Freddie with a vicious smirk on my face.

"Oh Come on now! Give me a break. I am not that stupid now! Besides, I am not looking around, I'm on a sabbatical leave, a journey of abstinence my friend!" Freddie said with some hesitation.

"For how long 10 days? Prove me wrong Freddie, and I'll go down on my knees asking for your forgiveness."

"Okay, enough of that Barry, how are you doing yourself?"

"Thanks for asking, I think I'm in love!"

"Say that again… in love? You? Did I hear you well?"

"Yeah! It's recent. She works with me in the office, actually she's my private secretary." I said.

"It sounds private alright!" Freddie said facetiously.

"She's 35 years old, very pretty and sexy! I felt it when I hired her 2 months ago. It smelled trouble and now I think I'm in love." I said

"How about her… tell me more and what is it that she found so special about you?" Freddie said to tease me.

"Oh Thanks! You don't think I'm worthy to be loved by a gorgeous women like her? I can tell you respectfully… she's not Jane. She's a very decent woman. She has two very young kids and was divorced a year ago. She finds me very special I want you to know! Her name is Melody, and she's quite different than hum… all the women I went out with." I said confidently.

"How many women, three?" Freddie asked ridiculously.

"Okay that's it… I won't tell you anything personal any more."

"Come on Barry, I'm kidding! I'm so happy for you. I'd like to meet her, maybe she has a friend she can recommend." Freddie said.

"Oh, now you're interested right? Okay, you take us to a nice restaurant and you pay the bill."

"With pleasure, let's do it this Saturday, I am free." Freddie said. They finished their dinner chatting about their business, and then parted with a friendly hug.

Freddie received a call from one of his lawyers, James during the week, who said that they served the counter response to the court rejecting Jane's claims and asking for dismissal. He added that they did some investigation about Jane's background and it's not good. Freddie asked,

"Why? What did you find out James?"

"She belongs to a suspicious club that allegedly sponsors women like Jane to chase rich men. We could tell from Jane's choice of lawyers. These lawyers had represented other women in similar cases. The law firm is small but notorious for bullying their opponents; they could be a 'club' themselves? And, in many cases they succeeded to force clients to pay up, though they had no legal chance to win. They harass their opponents with threats and bodily harm sometimes." James said.

"So, what are you telling me that they might force us to pay up too?" Freddie asked.

"Yes, that's what I'm saying. First be careful if a stranger approaches you… or if you get harassed, by people you don't know. We'll dig further into the case, and will see how they legally respond or react when they know we're putting up a fight." James said.

"Ok thanks for telling me, James. Please keep me advised. I'll be careful." Freddie said before he hung up the phone.

***

Freddie went to the Fellowship center and heard a lecture given by a visiting senior monk from a monastery in Dharmasala, India where the Dalai Lama lives in exile since 1959, after his escape from the Tibet when the Chinese took over. The message was about the *Law of Dharma*, or the purpose in life. The message emphasized three points. First, learn how to meditate and connect with your higher self. Once you realize who you are, make a list of your talents, and the ultimate purpose is to use your talent to serve other people. Freddie thought silently:

> *"This looks like a tall order. Apparently my purpose in life was not only to succeed in business and to take care of my family needs? I ask myself if I already know who I am? No I don't! I also thought my talent is business-related, do I have*

other talents? And how am I to help others? What does that really mean?"

Freddie decided that going to these lectures and meditation lessons might not be sufficient. He started reading articles online related to these ideas. The more he read the more he realized how little did he know. It became evident that this new path he was considering to follow is a fairly long path and required a lot of perseverance and discipline. He doubted if he could achieve self-realization, the key to discovering other life values. In his state of questioning he was tempted to have a drink thinking it would take the edge off. He struggled to abstain, but his mind caved and he gave in to the bottle.

He was alone in the evening the same day of the Fellowship. He helped himself with three drinks then he noticed he was getting tipsy, not a good sign for someone who was seeking a better life. He obliged himself to stop drinking. He then took a shower and went to bed early. He was meeting Barry and Melody the next day.

Freddie invited Barry and his girl friend to a nice French restaurant in Midtown Manhattan. He was quite impressed with the personality of Melody and was eager to share his impressions with Barry later. She was a classy lady, a beautiful brunette and an average height. She looked quite compatible with Barry and they seemed to be quite happy together. She said to Freddie,

"Barry told me about your old friendship with him, and how you can rely on one another if any of you needed."

"That's true! I have given him few headaches lately, since my divorce and he's been quite tolerant. I am grateful to his being by my side when I needed him." Freddie said.

"Isn't that what good friends are for?" Melody responded.

"What's the latest with Jane? You can talk, Melody knows the story." I asked.

"It's not so good! My lawyers found out that she could be part of a notorious group of lawyers that sponsors girls, to suck more money rich married men and pretend they are loyal girl friends. Jane seemingly was part of that 'club'. Now I understand why she always asked me for more money... I had no clue that she was playing such a game. My lawyers warned me that if I—I don't cooperate and give her something decent they might threaten or hurt me. Her lawyers orchestrated the whole debacle um… despite an anticipated court's decision in my favor." Freddie said with concern.

"Wow! What a story! Will you call her and reason something out?" I asked.

"No, we are in a legal battle at the moment. Will see what happens first!"

"Be careful Freddie, these guys can play dirty, try your best to cut it short, and quick." I commented.

The rest of the evening went well and the conversation shifted to discuss other social and business matters. Melody told Freddie that she has a friend he might be interested to meet sometime soon. They walked out together and Freddie said good night and turned right to go back to his hotel.

On his way he thought it was about time he moved into an apartment, especially that the outlook to reconnect with his wife was not far-fetched. The hotel stay was getting to be boring and not homey. There was also the possibility he might even go to India, for a long period if the Fellowship did not bring him the desired improvement. He knew that his top priority in life was to be spiritually transformed, to discover true love and happiness. The question was how to go about it?

With his confused state of mind he stopped at the hotel bar for a nightcap to forget the unresolved issues of his life. He ended up having more than a few drinks and the concierge had to help him up to his suite. He crashed in bed with his clothes on and woke up three hours later, embarrassed and with a hangover. He took his clothes off, took a shower and went back to sleep.

***

Freddie got up at 10:00 am on Sunday morning and decided to stay in, to nurse his headache and reflect on his life condition. He ordered a pot of coffee and some toast and sat in his living room with his laptop. He spent the bulk of his day going through self-help articles and book recommendations. He also collected more information about potential monasteries of ashrams he might go to. He tried to meditate as he was taught but it did not mean much. He could not empty his mind form the disturbing thoughts that kept distracting him.

He sat up looking at the ceiling, and tossing with the idea whether he should call Jane, to ask about her intention behind the lawsuit. His advisors had told him not to talk to her. The first hearing was scheduled to take place in two days, and he decided to wait for the decision of the court on Tuesday. His lawyers filed a request to dismiss the case, as it had no legs to stand on. He wandered what could happen if Jane loses the case. Would she harass him, forget him, or would she collaborate with her 'shady' club to force him to pay? She knew where he worked and about his assets, where his family lived, and the hotel he was staying at.

He ordered lunch to be served in his room, took an afternoon nap and then put his jeans on to go for a walk in the park. It was a nice sunny spring day and he got tired staying alone in his suite.

***

The Park was buzzing with people. There were couples holding hands, parents with their children, individuals walking their dogs and others sitting on benches watching people going by. Freddie kept walking north and when got close to the Met Museum, he looked for his usual bench and found a young beautiful blonde woman occupying one end of it. All other benches were fully occupied. He asked her if he could sit on the other end and she nodded with a smile. After few minutes Freddie asked her if she regularly comes to the Park. She answered,

"No, it is my second day in New York… I came to visit from Madison, Wisconsin. I was at the museum all day, and came out to rest and get some sun. How about you?"

"I live here… I was just taking a walk in the Park. It's a nice day and here I am. My name is Freddie Rodman by the way um, what is yours?"

"My name is Anne…Anne Stevenson. I took a week off from my work to visit this bustling city of yours."

"Did you have a chance to see other landmarks besides the Museum, Anne?"

"No, not really… I want to see the Statue of Liberty, Ground Zero, and the Empire State building, among others."

"Good choices and if you like museums I am sure you heard about the MoMa, and the Guggenheim, near here. Where are you staying here? Um…Do you have friends in town?" Freddie asked.

"I am staying at a small hotel midtown and no, I don't have any friends here."

"You seem to be a nice lady, I am alone, getting divorced, and I would like to invite you to dinner, if you have nothing else to do." Freddie said eagerly.

"That's very nice of you, I would love to… you seem to be a nice man too." Anne said.

Freddie suggested they walk back towards the main entrance on 59th street. This way they could get to know a little more about each other. They stood up and that's when Freddie noticed how tall Anne was. She was 5ft 9in. tall and blessed with an amazing body completing her beautiful face with blue eyes and gorgeous lips. They walked slowly and he told Anne a bit about his work, when he left the house he lived in with his wife and two boys. He did not bring up the episode about Jane but mentioned he's doing some soul-searching now to get rid of his anger and guilt feelings.

Then he asked Anne about her story. She said,

"I am a psychoanalyst, I have a doctorate degree in psychology. I work on my own, and most of my patients are in troubled relationships. I am 32 years old and I started this practice 7 years ago. I am also divorced but have no children. Our marriage was short and ended two years ago. I am not in a relationship at the moment and I am glad I could take this week off my very busy schedule. Have you ever been in Madison?"

"Wow… what an impressive career! No, I haven't visited Madison yet, though I hear it's quite a civilized place that boasts of a high level of education thanks to its University of Wisconsin. And it's also known for its restaurants, lakes and beautiful parks." Freddie said.

"You're right on the dot there… I like it because it is not a big city like New York. It is quite charming and manageable with its 250,000 population… spread between four lakes." Anne responded.

"Are most of the girls in Madison tall and beautiful like you?" Freddie asked.

"I am flattered. Both my parents are descendants of Swedish immigrants, the reason for my height and hair color." Anne explained.

They spoke in general about the political situation in the country and Anne stated that Madison is a strong supporter of the Left politically, similar to your situation here in New York. She added that she finds New York quite an expensive place to live in, when compared to Madison. By the time they arrived at the main entrance it was around 6:30 pm and Freddie asked Anne,

"Would you prefer to eat early, or have a drink first?"

Anne smiled and said,

"I skipped lunch today and I wouldn't mind eating early, if it's OK with you." Freddie smiled back and pointed his finger out and said,

"Not at all, Um… let's go here to Cipriani, it's a good Italian restaurant. I'm sure they'll take us this early."

They crossed the street and walked over to the restaurant and a table for two was waiting for them by the window.

Freddie noticed how cool Anne was. She was laid back, attentive to him when he talked, and relaxed about the city surroundings. They had a glass of champagne as an aperitif and looked at the menu for a while. They placed their orders and Freddie chose a bottle of good red Italian wine. He felt comfortable with Anne and wished she lived in New York to become friends. He appreciated being with an educated and classy woman for a change. Anne started the conversation,

"Tell me Freddie, if you don't mind me asking. You mentioned earlier that um… you are going through a soul-searching journey, which is admirable by the way, do you care to—to tell me the reasons why?"

"No, not at all, as a psychoanalyst I am sure you are entitled to know and will quickly understand, and perhaps suggest few steps for me to follow…" Freddie replied with interest.

"I don't intend to analyze you, we're just talking as friends here and if you're uncomfortable um… we can talk about something else…" Anne explained.

"I would be honored to share my story with you and I would welcome any suggestions you may recommend…" Freddie added with a happy smile.

"OK then before you start, can you tell me a bit about your childhood?" Anne asked.

"I... I can't say that I had a very happy childhood. My father was too busy with work and my mother busy with her social life. I had my nanny and I—I did not get a lot of love and attention from my parents. That made me wonder why other kids were happier than me. I was the only child and could not understand why my parents ignored me. I must have carried that feeling throughout my adolescent and adult life. That also clarifies... why I did not understand what true love is all about when I married Matilda, my ex-wife." Freddie patiently explained.

Anne was silent for few seconds and then said,

"Hum... I fully understand what happened and if it is of any help to you, you are not the only one who had such a childhood... I can tell you about many other people I treated, with more miserable childhoods than yours. I come across this in my work all the time. Your situation is mild compared to others."

"That's good to know, are you saying I should not be concerned about my current guilt feelings?" Freddie asked.

"That's different... I know of many parents who had happy childhoods, yet felt very guilty leaving their kids. The guilt can be handled with time, and it—it eventually fades away. The issue here is about our understanding of what true love is... You did not experience it, and I can also tell you um... my ex-husband did not either. True love is—is unconditional love, similar to the love you have for your children. It has become um... a big issue among married couples nowadays. Individual demands are being imposed, especially when earlier expectations of—of what each initially wanted fade away." Anne professionally said.

"So what you are saying is that I was disappointed why my wife did not make up for the love that I missed from my mother?"

"Well, partly yes! But mainly it—it is you who did not appreciate the love your wife must have given you. Because you had not yet accepted why you did not get it from your mother... So, that is the reason many husbands end up blaming what they did not get from their mothers, on their wives... Then they start escaping and sleeping around, thinking they can get what they lack outside their marriage." Anne expounded more clearly.

"Wow Anne! You hit it right on! That's exactly what happened to me... and that's what I did." Freddie said with a sad look on his face.

"So, tell me what are you doing to enhance your process of soul-searching?"

"First, I stopped my relationship with a girl friend who triggered the process of my divorce… Then I started taking self-realization lectures and I learned how to meditate, at a Fellowship center here in the city. I even considered going to India to—to join a monastery or an ashram. I am still struggling with what I should do really!" Freddie factually stated.

"That's good! It's not an easy process. It's a good start. You need to persevere, and try to avoid escapes such as drinking or drugs, you know!" Anne said casually.

"What, are you a mind reader? Did any one tell you that I started drinking more heavily, since the separation?"

"Of course not, it is a common expectation when one feels wrong about something, or separated from his loved ones." Anne explained.

"This is amazing! I love to hear how you explain these things Anne…"

"Well, seven years of higher education, and seven years of practice taught me well… Thanks anyhow! I appreciate you listening to me, which I'm doing to understand better what you're going through." Anne said with a smile gracing her face.

"I'm so glad we met. I—I don't think it was pure coincidence. I believe Destiny meant for us to meet… I hope we can see each other again while you are still in town." Freddie said.

"As I told you I am free all evenings… and I'm so happy I met you too. I appreciate, and I enjoy your company. And I thank you for this wonderful evening, and this delicious meal."

"It is still early, is there anything you would like to see tonight? Would you like to go to a jazz club or something?" Freddie asked politely.

"Oh, I would love that, I love soft jazz. Are you up for it?" Anne asked.

"Of course I am, we can go to Blue Note… I'm sure they have a good program tonight. Which hotel are you staying in?"

"A boutique hotel called 'The Mansfield'."

"Don't tell me, it's on 44th street! Mine is on the same street, less than a block away from you, it's the 'Algonquin'… How often does this happen? So, let's take a taxi downtown to listen to some jazz." Freddie said delightfully.

They went to the club and stayed there till 11:00 pm. Freddie dropped her off at the hotel and said goodnight. They agreed to meet again, and he said he'd pick her up at 7:00 pm the next day. He had a short walk to his hotel feeling very happy to have met Anne, and wondered how such great women still exist. He slept pretty well that night and couldn't wait to tell Barry about it in the morning.

CHAPTER 4

Hope Vs. Despair

Freddie called me from his office the next day. He told me about meeting Anne. He was excited as if he found some stolen treasure. I listened patiently, but feeling good for him as well. Freddie asked me if I would like to meet her and we could have dinner the four of us tomorrow. I agreed, and that cheered him up. When Freddie hung up he took a pause to reflect on the time spent with Anne and thought,

> *"I cannot forget what Anne explained during dinner last night. She talked about the concept of 'True Love', which seemed to be a strange subject given that I had not literally experienced yet. I certainly shouldn't blame it on my parents any longer. It is what it is… and I am glad I can manifest this with my children. What I appreciated the most about Anne is that she was not judgmental, or curious about details. She was truly professional and gentle in her explanations. It's a pity she doesn't live around here. I am eager to hear her talk again. Oh, not to forget, she's so darn beautiful too."*

Freddie was in the lobby of her hotel at 7:00 pm sharp. He came straight from work and was still dressed in his suit and tie. Anne came out of the elevator a minute later, and she looked dazzling. She had a beautiful light green dress on, with a matching low-heeled shoes and a cute handbag. Her face was radiant in harmony with the rest of her features. Her smile was cheerful and welcoming.

Freddie approached her and kissed her on her right cheek. He had reserved a nice table at a close by French restaurant he frequented. They both expressed how happy they were to see each other again. On the way over, Anne told Freddie the places she visited during the day, and how glad she was to be in New York.

Once seated in the restaurant Freddie ordered a bottle of French wine and he held his glass to toast Anne, thanking her for bringing up the subject of True Love, which was missing in his life. Then he said

"Tell me please, I have always wanted to love the people around me, and I thought that would make me happy. Instead I ended up experiencing fear… and I ask myself, why am I here on this planet? How can I stay hopeful, while I—I continue my search to find my life purpose?"

Anne was touched by the admission of how he felt, and after few seconds she responded,

"Look! True Love is deeper than passion… It is calm and dwells on quality alone; it is wise and devotes itself to what is real, unique and long lasting. True love does not get tired from giving… The more love you give the more you receive back… Antoine Saint-exupery explained it clearly when he said 'when you go to the fountainhead, the more water you draw, the more abundant it flows.' In a way, and in order to really understand true love, you need to be spiritual."

"Anne… I can sit at your feet and listen to you all day. You are amazing, and I am so lucky to have met you… Tell me please how about true love in friendship?" Freddie asked.

"Jean de la Fontaine said, 'rare as true love, true friendship is rarer.' So, there you go! It's not easy to find true friends nowadays. Do you have a good friend Freddie?" Anne asked curiously.

"In fact I do. Barry and I have been best friends for more than 20 years… I go to him when I am in need of a shoulder to cry on. He's more solid than me. He's become my alter ego and my sounding board. I'd like to introduce you to him and his new girl friend… He'll tell you what a pain in the neck I'd been."

"Wow, that's impressive… from those qualities you can appreciate how true love should be like. True friendship is similar to true love, it can teach us um… how to be the best version of who we are. Yes, I'd like to meet him." Anne said eloquently.

"OK... I'll invite him and Melody to have dinner with us tomorrow night, how about that? Now, tell me more about yourself." Freddie wanted to know.

"As I said earlier, lately it's been work... work... and work. I met few fellows in social circles lately, but none of them left a good impression on me. It's not that I am frigid, or have no interest in men, it's just um... it hasn't happened yet. I have a solid good friend though, an ex-colleague I met, before I started my own practice... she's a psychologist too, and still working with the same group. We see each other on weekends and some weekday evenings. I value our true friendship a great deal!"

"That's good to know Anne, at least you kept an open door to true friendship and may be one day you'll meet your soul-mate." Freddie said.

"Oh no! wait a minute, a soul mate is not what I am looking for... soul- mates are not the answer to searching for true love. They are not eternal... as in a true love relationship. You are your own soul and the focus should be on nurturing your own soul. Souls are not to be shared with another mate. You may romantically say 'I met my soul-mate' but such relationships don't normally last long. Every soul has its own vibrational source of energy, and it is very likely that two souls may clash, um... once they find they are on two different vibrational streams. If you are looking for true love, then look for a 'life partner', someone you can happily share the rest of your life with. I'll stop now, I talk too much..." Anne was on a roll and the wine helped to loosen her up.

Freddie smiled and begged her to keep on talking,

"Please continue... I love it when you explain such good stuff."

"OK... if you insist, allow me then to read to you an excerpt of what my favorite poet and philosopher Khalil Gibran, wrote in his famous book, The Prophet. Anne pulled out her smartphone from her handbag and found some excerpts she had downloaded from the book, and began to read it poetically:

> *"Let there be spaces in your togetherness and let the winds of the heavens dance between you,*
> *Love one another but make not a bond of love: Let it be a moving sea between the shores of your souls.*
> *Fill each other's cup but drink not from one cup.*

Give one another of your bread but eat not from the same loaf.
Stand together yet not too near together: For the pillars of the temple stand apart, and the oak tree and the cypress grow not in each other's shadow."

Anne read it slowly, which she almost knew by heart, while she was looking at Freddie straight at his eyes and smiling throughout the flow of her narration. She paused for 10 seconds and did not utter a word, admiring the reaction on Freddie's face with his jaws dropped and his misty eyes staring in space. When he cooled down he said,

"Anne can you please forward this to me? … here is my number." He said nothing for a while. Then he said,

"This poet is my hero… I want to buy this book and memorize it if I can. It summarizes all what I—I need to know about love, relationships and souls." Freddie was enthused.

"I'll text you all that… I just wanted you to know why the term 'soul-mate' does not resonate well with me." Anne said quietly.

"Of course! I fully understand… and thanks again for this crash course in enlightenment." Freddie responded.

"I am delighted you enjoy our conversation, and I appreciate your attention to my words." Anne said softly.

"Are you kidding me, you are the best teacher… ever! I feel so uninformed next to you. How can I reciprocate to your generous attention to my troubled life?" Freddie admitted.

"Come on now! let us talk about something else, how about you taking me to a Broadway musical one evening? That will be my compensation… OK?" Anne said with a mild laughter.

"It'll be my pleasure my dear! I'll check what's we find for Thursday, because tomorrow we plan to be with Barry and Melody."

"It sounds great, thanks. Do you want to go dancing tonight to lighten up some?" Anne suggested.

"OK… let's do that." Freddie asked for the check when they finished the meal and took a taxi downtown to a dancing club he knew. They went to the PH-D lounge, a classy rooftop dance club known for its hip-hop music.

They arrived early and found good seats looking at the night skyline of Manhattan. Anne loved it and they had fun together for two hours, then called it a night around 11:30 pm. They took a taxi back and Freddie asked Anne if she cared for a nightcap at his hotel. She agreed while feeling tipsy herself. They went straight up to his suite. She ran to use to the bathroom and when she walked out she noticed the good-looking suite and said,

"Wow! you live here?"

"Yupp… it's been my home for the last several months. I am now thinking of moving to a apartment, as the chances of going back home are nil. What can I get you from the minibar?"

"I'll be happy with a beer, I am thirsty from all the drinking and dancing. I want to thank you for giving me such a great time… Meeting you has been the highlight of my trip." Anne said.

"Happy to hear that Anne, it's a pity you don't live around here. I think we can be great together."

"I feel the same way, we'll see what the future has in store for us."

Freddie gave her the drink and sat next to her on the sofa. She held his hand and thanked him again. He smiled back at her and asked if he could kiss her. She did not say a word, and moved closer to him and kissed him passionately. Then she said, "I've been wanting to kiss these gorgeous lips of yours!"

One thing led to another and few minutes later they found themselves taking a shower together to cool off the heated making-out session in the living room. They giggled with laughter like two young lovers excited about their first love making adventure.

***

Freddie and Anne woke up late the next morning, showered and ordered breakfast from room service. They expressed how they both enjoyed sharing the same bed together and Anne repeated her appreciation to be with him. Freddie asked her,

"When do you fly back?"

"Saturday afternoon, from La Guardia airport."

"Can you extend your stay another week? He asked again.

"I wish I can but I have a full schedule next week… I must go back." Anne said regrettably.

"I'm going to miss you very much you know?"

"Me too! You are a wonderful man and you have a very generous heart. We can be regularly in touch by phone or Skype. I am available if you need to talk… or ask me questions. I wish you the best, and I hope we can meet again soon."

Freddie moved closer to hug her and to thank her for an amazing time. They got dressed and Anne wanted to go ahead with her plans to see more attractions in New York, while Freddie had planned to go to his office. They agreed to meet again at 6:30 pm and have dinner with Barry and Melody at 7:00. He told her to call him if she needs anything during the day. They walked out of the hotel together, and she went to her hotel less than 200 feet away to change her clothes.

There was a message waiting for Freddie in his office to call the lawyers. He called and spoke with James who told him that the judge dismissed the case and Jane's lawyers were not happy. James told him to be careful as they may not easily walk away from coercing you to pay. Freddie asked James,

"What kind of money were they hoping to get?"

"A couple of big ones?" James said.

"What, Millions?" Freddie shouted.

"Yeah, I told you they play dirty… They could have settled for one million, but not less. That's their game. It's not the first time they do that. They had some legal success in the past, though different cases were their clients lived with their rich men for more than a year. We're lucky you didn't do that. But, they are capable of harassing you outside the court… They have a bunch of tough guys who do the leg work for them if you know what I mean!" James elaborated.

"What do you mean? Don't be bashful, tell me."

"You may receive threatening phone calls asking for money, or you'll regret it if you don't agree… stuff like that." James said

"Wow, are we living in a jungle still or what?"

"Come on, don't be naive! Keep me advised if you hear from any stranger and will take from there."

***

Freddie wished he didn't have this conversation with his lawyer. He had spent a wonderful time with Anne, and the conversation with James was an anti-climax to the hopes he had developed from his new friendship with Anne. He called me and bothered me at work. It was a short conversation during which he told me about the great time he had with Anne and the news from his lawyer. I told him to take it easy and hope nothing serious will happen. We agreed not to discuss this Jane subject in front of the ladies.

Freddie spent the rest of the day confused and he wondered if he should spend the afternoon with Anne instead. He considered her a new crutch that he can lean on. She knew how to make him relax. His mind raced with contrasting thoughts and images that shifted between the realms of fear and love, hope and despair. He asked himself

> *"Am I falling in love, or was last night just a brief moment of pleasure that would not develop into a serious relationship?*
> *How should I pursue the relationship with Anne after she leaves to go home? Is there a chance for us to be together one day?*
> *Why should there be a continued conflict between the pleasure of meeting Anne and the headaches that Jane keeps giving me? What am I supposed to learn from these experiences? Is suffering the basic condition before enlightenment, as the Buddhists teach?*
> *How am I on the road to awareness and self-realization?"*

These questions floated in Freddie's head all morning. He had a luncheon meeting with a real estate developer and he thought he would call Anne to see if he could join her wherever she was doing around 3:00 pm. He wanted to take advantage of the short time left and see her as much as possible.

He called her after lunch and she told him she was planning to visit the Museum of Modern Arts. They agreed to meet at 2:45 pm at the entrance on 53rd street.

***

Anne was happy to see Freddie who was dressed up while she was in casual clothes, a pair of jeans and a white shirt. Her tight jeans showed her firm body and long legs. They hugged, he bought the tickets and agreed to go straight to the impressionist art section. They both liked the works of Van Gogh, Monet, Picasso, Cezanne and the like. After an hour admiring these masterpieces, particularly the 'starry night' by Van Gogh, they went to the café on the terrace for some coffee. They sat quietly and Anne noticed that Freddie was anxious about something. She asked him,

"What's on your mind Freddie, you seem to be pre-occupied?"

"Is suffering a pre-requisite to happiness?" Freddie let it out.

Anne looked at him and smiled. She asked him,

"Is this um… what you learnt from your Buddhist lectures?"

"Yeah, but I didn't understand it well."

"I see! Well here we go again, another serious talk! Allow me to say that Life is… constantly changing, and causes suffering to come along with it. Often, moments of happiness suddenly disappear and that causes suffering. Our experience these last few days is a live example of that. We are having great moments of happiness together now… and then Bang! It disappears when we part ways in different directions." Anne explained.

"Yes, but only for a while, as we intend to meet again, no?" Freddie wanted to correct her.

"True, but the period of separation can be hard and unpleasant. It is ironic that the only 'constant' in life is 'change'. In fact, one moment is always chased by another moment that comes along fast on its heels. We try to prolong and enhance our moments of pleasure in life, but there is always something else that comes up… and that may cause us to suffer."

"Are you saying, Anne um… that life is a dance between desirable and unpleasant moments all the time?" Freddie asked.

"Yes, It is a universal truth of life. None of us —wealthy, wise or powerful – is an exception. We all feel pain, we all lose loved ones, we all get ill, and we all die." Anne emphasized.

"Why does uncertainty of the future make me so anxious? Freddie asked.

"We feel threatened and insecure about what might appear around the next corner… That is why we become anxious. This is due to our intrinsic instability, as human beings."

"Why do I feel a sense of meaninglessness in my life?" Freddie confessed.

"Sometimes, we go through unbearable periods of self-doubt and angst about who we are… That is why Buddha said that suffering is an experience of the mind or the mental activity that causes misery. That is why in all his teachings Buddha teaches self- realization and relief of the mind, and meditation was his key… to quiet the mind." Anne calmly explained.

"Again, my dear professor, thank you for this new course in enlightenment. Perhaps I should pursue the lectures in the Fellowship and continue with my daily meditations." Freddie concluded.

"That would definitely help! Be strong and don't be fragile… especially in moments of difficulty. Be aware of what's going on and rely on your intuition… Have faith in your self, and allow the Universe to reveal the Truth in your daily life."

Freddie thanked her and they had another hour before they needed to get ready for their dinner. Anne said she'd seen what she wanted from the museum and they decided to walk back to the hotel, less than 10 blocks away.

On the way back Freddie told Anne about Jane and what she might do to hurt him. Anne listened and had nothing to say other than the words, "Be strong and don't be afraid".

He dropped Anne off at her hotel and said he'll pick her up in one hour, and to dress casually. When he arrived at his place, he decided to take out a sheet of paper and jot down the main points he learned from the conversation with Anne. The more he spent time with Anne the more he was attracted to her. He found her to be gorgeous all around, physically, emotionally and intellectually. He wondered how he could sustain this relationship after her return?

***

Freddie picked her up to meet Barry and Melody for dinner. The restaurant was not far so they decided to walk. He told Anne that he was able to find two tickets to see the 'Phantom of the Opera' on Thursday. She was elated as she had wanted to see this musical for many years. He also told her Barry knows about Jane and the shady group she's with. He asked Anne,

"I noticed that you didn't comment at all when I told you about Jane and what she's capable of doing. Why you went silent on me?"

"Freddie…Freddie, this past experience of yours doesn't interest me… what can I say? You chose to be with her and you have to bear the consequences of your decision. We all make mistakes sometimes." Anne said factually.

"You're right. I'll handle it the best I can. At least I was able to move her out of my life. I won't bother you with her story anymore." Freddie softly stated.

"It is not a matter of bothering me Freddie, it's a—a situation that I cannot help you with. It dwells on the negative, and I try to stay away from negative affairs, please don't misconstrue my intentions." Anne explained convincingly.

"No problem my dear, I got your point!" Freddie said just before they reached the restaurant.

They walked in together holding hands. I saw them from the table I was at, with Melody. I waved, and Freddie walked over with Anne. I stood up to introduce my self to Anne, who was almost my height, and then I introduced her to Melody. We all sat down and Freddie ordered a bottle of champagne to kick off the evening.

Anne spoke first and she said to me,

"Barry, I heard good things about you from Freddie, old friends.. uh?"

"Old friends alright… I don't know how he put up with me all this time." I responded.

"Don't believe him Anne, he meant the contrary. I always gave him a hard time… especially the last year or so." Freddie intercepted.

"Freddie tells me you're a psychologist and he's happy you gave him good advice." I said.

"Freddie is a very intelligent man and does not need my advice. He's just working on some emotional and spiritual aspects of his life, he's been through a lot lately. I'm sure he'll overcome all his fears soon." Anne said in Freddie's defense.

"Congratulations! You figured him out pretty well already. I've known him for more than 20 years… and I still can't figure him out yet… I guess because you're an expert in this field." I said.

"Hey Melody, don't worry! He will never figure you out either. He's slow! Remain an enigma and let him guess… he's not fully with it, upstairs!" Freddie said jokingly.

They all laughed and continued sipping on their champagne and looking at the menu. Melody asked Anne,

"How long do you intend to stay in New York? And do you like our city?"

"Unfortunately I have to go back this Saturday, and I like New York very much indeed. Freddie has been a great companion… and we plan to see a musical tomorrow. He spoils me well." Anne answered.

They placed their meal orders and the women chatted together, while Freddie and I were catching up on the latest. He whispered in my ear how much he liked Anne and asked me what do I think? I gave him thumps up, discretely. Then Freddie said half-seriously,

"Anne is considering to move to New York, don't you think she'll have a great practice here? I'll be her first patient!"

"Is this true?" Melody asked.

"He's kidding, can't you tell?" Anne responded while poking his side.

"No seriously Anne, would you consider it? This city would love to have you here. I have vacant offices that I can offer you space rent-free… Barry and I will refer you to many potential patients, most of our friends badly need your help, we all need your help actually… you're the best!" Freddie said enthused.

There were few moments of silence and every one was looking at Anne waiting for her to respond. Few seconds later she said,

"Freddie… you are very sweet to ask me to consider. And, I know that you may not be kidding. I told you about my very busy schedule in Madison. I can't just turn my back on my patients and leave. I spent 7 years building up my practice… do you want me to start from scratch again? I am not hum… prepared to do that, sorry!" Anne said factually.

"I hear you, at least I tried folks!" Freddie looked at Melody and me, when he said that.

"This tells me that he really likes to have you around Anne… Isn't it Freddie?" I said.

"You said it Barry… I'm being selfish I guess! I may have to fly to Madison every week to continue being her patient." Freddie said.

"That's a good idea… now you're talking. It's a little more than a two-hour flight. And, I won't charge you any fees… how about that? I can also see you on weekends as an exception. Will you do it?" Anne intended to trap Freddie.

"You caught me there, Anne. It's just that I like your company very much, that's all!" Freddie admitted.

"You two are so sweet and I'm sure you'll keep in touch." I said.

They changed the conversation to more general subjects and continued to talk and laugh, enjoying the rest of the evening.

***

Anne had two more days left in New York before she returns home. Freddie took her to see the musical, which she thoroughly enjoyed and was grateful to see. On Friday afternoon he accompanied her to see the statue of Liberty and walked around the Wall Street area and pointed out to the building where I work.

They had dinner and then spent the night together at Freddie's suite. No personal issues were discussed and the atmosphere was light and relaxing. They went to bed early and Anne remembered that Freddie's two boys would be there at 10:00 am Saturday morning. They had an early breakfast, and Freddie was sad to see her go. They thanked one another for the wonderful week they had together and promised to keep in touch.

CHAPTER 5

New Threats and Demands

Anne sent a text message Saturday evening informing Freddie that she was at home already, and thanked him again for his hospitality and the great time she had with him. The weekend with the children was delightful and Freddie was able to share with them an extra dose of love. He remembered the true love discussions he had with Anne and he was happy to demonstrate its true meaning freshly with the two boys.

On Sunday evening, and right after the departure of his children, Freddie's mobile phone rang. He picked it up and heard a strange hoarse voice telling him,

"You have 48 hours to come up with two million dollars cash… Will call you when and where to deliver the package. If you don't cooperate you'll regret it." Then the caller hung up.

Freddie sat down in his chair, frozen and shaken. His mobile was dropped on the floor and his mind was racing with all kinds of negative and unpleasant thoughts. He remembered the talk with Anne that he has to be strong and now allow fear to rule over him. He picked the device to check if there was any ID number of the caller and there was none. He figured that this was what the lawyer, James told him to expect. He called James right away and told him what happened. James said,

"It's best you don't answer the phone if the caller cannot be identified. Just stay calm, and it's useless to call the police yet. The call was not recorded and you have no evidence to prove the threat… Try not to walk the streets alone and it's best to take a taxi to work and back. Stay in, and don't go out at night. Don't call Jane and accuse her of anything. Stay cool and will see how this story evolves."

"Fine... I will follow your advice. But, are you sure there is nothing else you can do on your part?" Freddie asked.

"Like what?"

"Like calling the other lawyers and explain to them that you are aware of their moves and um... ask them to stop this harassment?" Freddie suggested.

"It's not a common practice between lawyers... let me ask my partners and will let you know if it's worth the effort. Will call you tomorrow, goodnight."

***

I received a phone call from Freddie on Monday morning. He told me about the threat and his conversation with the lawyer. He asked me if I have any ideas what to do. I answered,

"It's a pity you can't have long moments of joy for too long! You either lay low and see what happens next, or you hire a bodyguard to accompany you wherever you go. No wait... I have a better idea. We both know whose behind all this. Nothing happens without Jane's approval, right?" It's better you hire a private eye to follow her moves or to bug her communications somehow... I have a friend who knows of a very good one. I think it is worth contacting him. How about that? I'll text you his name and number shortly. It's best you call him."

"Fine Barry, I'll call him as soon as possible. Thanks, and we'll talk later!"

Freddie called Simon Trendent, the private detective at the number he received and they arranged a meeting in Simon's office to explain the situation in person. Freddie explained the story from the beginning of the relationship, the court case, the shady club she works with, and the recent phone call her received from a stranger. He showed him two photos of Jane from his device, gave him her home address and the smartphone number and brand she uses. He also gave him her fixed line number in her apartment. His main question was to check if there could be some evidence that she was colluding with her lawyers or the shady club, or even the guy that called.

Simon had Freddie sign an official agreement for the assignment at hand and said he will start the investigation right away and will revert with any relevant news.

***

Freddie was not comfortable before he went to sleep that night. He thought about calling Anne to cheer him up but he decided it is too soon to bother her. It was around 10:00 o'clock at night. He took a shower and then his phone rang. It was Anne. He was glad to hear her voice and said,

"I wanted to call you but I thought I would be bothering you… how are you, and thank you for calling me." Freddie said.

"I am fine. I had a hectic day at the office. I have many messages to respond to, and my schedule for the week is full. It's going to be a hectic time ahead… How about you, anything new?" Anne asked.

"The weekend with the kids was great, they noticed that I was a happier person than usual. I couldn't tell them that I owe it to you, the angel who enlightened me with her gracious presence and company. I just said that um… I love them dearly, and kept hugging them every chance I had. Soon after they left Sunday afternoon, I had a little scare. I received a threatening call regarding the situation you don't want to hear about, I am handling it as best as I can." Freddie said.

"What do you mean threatened? Now you have to tell me!" Anne insisted.

"It was a call from a stranger, hum… demanding $2 Million to be delivered within 48 hours, or else 'I'll regret it'. First I was shaken by the threat, then I remembered your advice to be strong, and that's what I am doing." Freddie explained.

"Are you sure it is your ex-girl friend behind this?" Anne asked.

"Quite sure, yes… she is part of a shady group whose job is to perform such charades. Anyhow, please drop it from your mind… let's talk about something more positive." Freddie said to change the subject.

"I miss you already, you spoiled me with your love and generosity." Anne said happily. Freddie appreciated her words and said,

"I miss you too, and I am glad I sat next to you on the bench in the park. I believe it was meant for us to meet. Your affection, and your wisdom have truly touched me deep within. I even wrote down what I could remember from your sweet words and explanations. I miss looking at your beautiful face when you talk… and your beautiful body when you walk."

"Wow, I didn't know you are a poet too! That's very sweet of you to say. Are you able to focus on your work despite the unexpected call?" Anne asked trying to go back to the same subject.

"I'm trying my best. I have good staff though." Freddie said.

"What exactly do you do, I never asked you?"

"I own and manage properties in Manhattan, and in other boroughs of the city. I inherited this from my father um… when he died few years ago. It keeps me busy."

"So you're a real estate tycoon, that's why your ex-girl friend is asking for so much money, right?" Anne said.

"Well! Now you know. I won't let her have it… that's for sure." Freddie said confidently.

"Good… just look after yourself and I wish you a good night's rest."

"You too sweet lady… I'll call you tomorrow and thanks for your call. Good night!"

Freddie felt much better after this brief talk with Anne and he went to bed hoping she'll visit him in his dreams.

***

When Freddie woke up Tuesday morning, his phone rang and the call had no ID. He did not answer. It rang again, and again he did not answer. He was nervous, he sat up in bed closed his eyes and prayed,

> *"Please God let these people leave me alone. Why do I have this continued conflict in my life? For how long do I have to suffer for the mistakes I've done? Why has the last year been a shift back and forth from light to darkness? I ended up not with the people I love, my family, nor with decent friends like Barry and Anne. Why should a stranger threaten me and demand a ransom? Do I deserve such a tiring burden? I want to laugh and have fun! I want to feel light and alive! Oh God, I ask for forgiveness, and please show me the way to what I should do next!"*

He felt better that he prayed, that he surrendered his fate to the Universe. He showered and got dressed to go to the office by taxi.

An hour later Simon called him and said,

"Hi, I just got back from where Jane lives… I parked my surveillance car outside opposite her apartment, which is in on the first level above the street. I sat there since 8:00 and I listened with my special equipment to her phone conversations with some people. I recorded two conversations that I thought were suspicious, and I am getting them analyzed. One of them drew my attention… it referred to a man telling Jane 'he made the call as scheduled on Sunday, but no one answered his calls this morning'. We don't know what that meant but will dig more into it and will let you know."

"Simon, wait a minute… I had two unidentified phone calls this morning and I did not answer, I bet you it's him… the same guy who called me on Sunday and demanded the money." Freddie said excited.

"Well, that could be it. We know we have her voice on the phone but we could not decipher the other voice as clearly. We need more evidence I'm afraid!" Simon concluded.

"How about the other call you recorded, Simon?" Freddie asked.

"It was much shorter… a man called her and asked 'any news?' And her answer was simply 'I'm on the job.' Simon explained.

"Simon listen, that could be a member of the 'club'… the shady group that sponsors her."

"I have them both recorded. If we go to court we'll um… oblige her to disclose the identity of the people she was talking to." Simon explained.

"I see! Please keep at it and let me know. Thanks!" Freddie said hoping they're getting closer to catch her.

***

Freddie updated his lawyer, James about the conversation with Simon. They agreed there is some hope now that she could be caught.

"How about the fact I did not pick up the phone… when it rang twice this morning.? Besides, he demanded the money on Sunday to be available Tuesday, which is today? What should I do, hide?" Freddie asked.

"Again don't walk back home… take a taxi. Also ask Simon to give us a copy of his report and the recordings… will see if we can use them to file an assumptive case with the court."

"What do you mean by 'assumptive'?"

"We assume that she's guilty, until she can prove she's innocent." James said.

"But isn't this a European law, and it's the opposite here?" Freddie noted.

"Yeah, may be! but it's worth the buzz it will create… and put some fear in them. Besides, we may have enough evidence from her voice on the phone, which she cannot deny, and she has to explain the reason for the conversations. So we may have a chance to trap her, will see!"

"OK…will ask him. Meanwhile, how is the divorce case developing?"

"We're having some progress. Matilda is agreeing to go to 40% of the net assets and asks for $15k monthly alimony and $5K child support, plus the house and all belongings. So it is getting better. I suggest we go back with 30%, $10k alimony and $4k child support. She can keep the house and her alimony stops if she remarries or lives with another man. Oh… I almost forgot, she wants you to pay for the boy's education through high school and college." James explained.

"How about my visitation rights? I want the boys for dinner with me once a week, every Thursday for example… and minimum two weeks vacation with me during their summer vacation. That's very important, anyhow please keep me advised and as I said um… I want to settle." Freddie demanded.

"Noted, will keep you posted!"

***

I had a call from Freddie telling me the latest developments. I was happy to hear about the progress in the settlement negotiations with Matilda and I appreciated his decision to conclude a fair settlement. I could not tell him what could happen next regarding the unanswered calls in the morning and I told him to keep looking behind his shoulder. Freddie also briefed me on the two recordings by the private eye and the consideration by the lawyers to sue Jane.

I then asked him,

"What kind of relationship do you plan to have with Anne, by the way?"

"What do you want me to say? You know me… I easily fall for a great woman like her… It's a pity she doesn't live here. We spoke yesterday and had a sweet conversation, though not long… She said she missed me and thanked me again for my 'love and generosity'. I also told her about the threatening call I received and she was concerned." Freddie briefed Barry.

"Freddie, you're in the midst of a tough situation that you need to resolve first. The ghost of Jane is still haunting you… besides, you have not settled with Matilda, and don't forget your responsibility of work and your employees… Do you have enough energy to pursue a relationship with Anne um… on top of all this? I challenged Freddie.

"You don't understand Barry, her presence in my life lightens my load and cheers me up. It makes me forget about ashrams and monasteries abroad. She's the best guru I—I could have. Besides, she has a good head on her shoulder, and a warm loving heart. In a way, I think I'm lucky she appeared in my life um… in the midst of all these headaches." Freddie said defensively.

"Fine you do what you think is best for you, for whatever it is worth, both Melody and me thought very highly of her… She's quite a catch, if you know what I mean!" I said truthfully.

"So now you changed your mind eh? A minute ago you hum… you told me she could be a burden and—and now you say she's a great catch? What is your truthful position in this case?" Freddie asked me.

"Honestly, I don't know! She would be the perfect lady for you if you had a clean slate already. I suggest you keep in touch with her without any rush for a commitment, and once you clean your act on both fronts -- Jane and Matilda-- you could then get more serious about her." I said as a true friend.

"OK… I buy that! I will definitely tread this road slowly, and focus on—on getting out of my current conflicting issues first. Always a pleasure to talk to you and many thanks!" Freddie said before he hung up with his best friend.

***

Around 7 pm in the evening, Freddie was looking forward to go home and call Anne. He went down before it got very dark and stood on the curb outside his building waiting for a taxi to come by. He was shocked when a black van suddenly stopped right by him and two big guys came out of the side door, masked and dressed in black. They grabbed him and forced him inside the van. They handcuffed him and put a black hood over his head. He did not scream or shout at them and remained silent for a minute while the van speeded down the road. He then nervously asked them,

"Who are you, and why are you doing this? What do you want?"

There was no reply. He asked them again,

"Where are you taking me? Please talk to me.!"

"Shut up… and you know very well what we want… where is the money and why didn't you answer your phone in the morning?" One guy said. His voice was similar to the voice of the one who first called him on Sunday.

"So what, you are going kill me now, because I was not available to talk?" Freddie asked.

"No, we will not kill you… not yet. We want the money first. We will just punish you a little." The same guy said.

Freddie had no idea where they were taking him. He guessed that the van was crossing a bridge from the noise of the wheels on the track. He figured they were taking him either to New Jersey or to Queens. Twenty minutes later the car stopped in what sounded like a scrapyard. They took him out and one guy started beating him with a baseball bat on his belly and his back. Freddie fell on the ground and felt a severe pain in his chest. The tough guy said,

"This is just to remind how serious we are… Next time you answer your phone, and have the money ready at the time and place we tell you." Then they picked him up from the ground and put him in the van and drove. Ten minutes later they stopped again, and dropped him off in front of a hospital emergency entrance. He still had the hood over his head and felt dizzy. They unlocked his handcuffs off and drove away very fast. He took the hood off but couldn't take a look at the van's license plate. He was focusing on his pain and dragged himself towards the entrance.

He was rushed into the treatment room by the entrance. Few minutes later he saw a doctor and two nurses looking at him. He fainted and didn't regain his consciousness for about three minutes. He later saw them wrapping his chest all around and the doctor spoke and told him he had fractured ribs. Freddie could hardly talk from pain. They gave him painkillers and obliged him to stay in the hospital for the night. They wanted to check him further to ensure he had no internal bleeding. He gave the nurse my name and number and asked her to call me, Barry.

The nurse called me and said that she was calling on behalf of Freddie Rodman. She gave me a brief description of his condition. I took the name and address of the hospital in Queens and took a taxi to go see him. I was there 30 minutes later and found Freddie in a semi-private room on his back, with light bruises on his face and arms and a big white wrap around his chest. Freddie was half-awake and managed to explain to me briefly what happened.

I felt sorry for him. I was the brother he never had, practically his only family now. His mother didn't care and his wife was estranged and he was alone.

I stayed with him for an hour. The sedatives put him to sleep early. I told the nurse that I'd come and see him in the morning. Before Freddie fell asleep he showed me Anne's number and asked me to call Anne and tell her what happened, the reason why he couldn't call as promised. I did what Freddie asked me to do when I got home and I reassured Anne that he's okay and not to worry. He also asked me to call Simon and the lawyers in the morning and tell them also what happened.

***

Freddie woke up feeling strong pain in his ribs' cage. He was given painkillers after his breakfast, which he could not eat. They took him for x-rays and MRI to check if he had any internal bleeding. The results were negative and he was to be discharged that morning. He was told to rest without movement for a whole week. Freddie checked his mobile and found a text message from his manager John. It read,

"Hi Boss, Stephanie from accounting called me last night and told me she saw you were picked up by some guys. I hope it's not serious. If it helps she noted the following plate number... Let me know if you need my help. John"

I went to see Freddie at 9:00 am and was told he can go home. They took him down in a wheel chair and I took him to his hotel. On the way over he showed me the text message from John and asked me to forward it to Simon and the lawyers, which I did right away. I left him to rest by 10:00 am and went to work. I told Freddie that I spoke to the people he asked me to do, and I'd come to see him after work.

Simon sent him a text message saying he's working on the message from Barry, and he'll come to see him in the early afternoon. James called and said that they have a stronger case now against Jane, especially with the license plate of the van that Barry sent him and Simon is now investigating. Freddie rested all morning, had some soup for lunch and then awaited the arrival of Simon to see him.

Simon arrived and Freddie asked the concierge to bring him up and open the door for him as he could not move easily. Simon started and said,

"The good news is that we now have the identity of the owner of the van and his photo. His name is Marco Donneti. Look at it and see if you recognize it. Freddie looked hard and said,

"It's possible that… he could be the man that spoke to me in the van but I cannot guarantee it… it was dark by the time I was picked up. I can say 70% it's him. Did you check his record?" Freddie asked.

"Yes of course, he is um… a big man about 6ft2 and lives in Queens. He has a record for several felonies with the police… and he was jailed once for a year, hurting a man in an alley. I am going to ask my detective friend at the police department in Queens to interrogate him. He's waiting for my call after our meeting here." Simon said.

"What if he's the one, what happens next?" Freddie asked.

"First, he'll be put behind bars… and will be asked to cooperate and inform the police who hired him. If he does, and reveals that it is Jane or her group… your lawyers will press charges against them and the court should rule in you favor and punish them." Simon said.

"Will he call me again?" Freddie asked.

"I very much doubt it, once he's interrogated this afternoon he'll lay low." Simon assured him.

"Thanks Simon, please call me with what you hear!".

"You bet I will, stay well and rest." Simon said before he left.

***

Freddie sent a message to Anne apologizing for not calling her yesterday as promised. He wrote that he's now resting at the hotel. He had few fractured ribs causing him pain in his chest but should be better in a week. Call me after work please. He then went back to sleep after taking two painkillers, and was awakened at 5pm by the phone ring. It was Simon. He right away said,

"The guy confessed, he said it was Jane Neiman who hired him. He agreed to testify in the court. The police told him if his story holds true, they would notify the judge, and request a merciful sentence… in return to his cooperation. Meanwhile he stays behind bars until the police in Manhattan interrogate Jane and may be arrest her."

"OK, that makes me feel better! Is your detective friend hum… coordinating with the Manhattan police now?" Freddie asked.

"Yeah, he started already, and most probably Jane will be visited still this afternoon… You can't procrastinate in such situations." Simon said.

"I appreciate the way you're handing this case Simon… Thanks, and you'll let me know please."

I went up to Freddie's suite around 5:30 and saw him looking at the ceiling. I got an extra key from the reception, which he authorized. As soon as I walked in Freddie said,

"They got the guy who kidnapped me. He confessed that it was Jane that hired him… He's behind bars now in Queens and the Manhattan Police will interrogate Jane this evening still."

"Well… well that's fast and good to hear. How does that make you feel?" I asked.

"Better, though the pain is excruciating… I can hardly move my upper body."

"I spoke to Matilda and told her what you went through." I said

"Why?"

"She's still your wife my friend… and the mother of your children. I thought she should know." I explained.

"How did she take it?"

"She felt sorry for you and wished you well."

"Okay, Thanks! How's Melody?" Freddie asked.

"She's fine and she'll be happy to hear that your suffering will not all go in vain, now that you told me. Did you speak with Anne?" I asked.

"No, not yet, I sent her a text and asked her to call me this evening. Barry, these guys could have killed me… I was scared. Do I deserve this?" Freddie wondered when he asked me.

"First, they wouldn't have killed you, they wanted your money and you did not follow through on their request, so they decided to send you a stronger message. What did you expect, that you're dealing with civilized people? They are unintelligent savages and look now how they fell in their own trap.

"Do you deserve it you ask? Of course not, but it is what it is. I'm sure there is a big lesson for you to learn here. We all make conscious decisions in life that we regret later. So, don't think negative, and be grateful for what you have. That's all!" I expounded philosophically.

"I hear you! Except for the few days I spent with Anne, I've been living in fear… isn't that a shame for someone my age?" Freddie complained.

"Listen! We all go through tough times occasionally. You're not alone, but stop being afraid, no one will really hurt you. You're just going through an experience of finding out what true life is all about and find out what you want and… who you are as a person." I philosophized again.

"Talking about finding out who I am, I've been thinking. If it doesn't work out with Anne, I may go to India or the Tibet or wherever… to cleanse my soul and learn how to love myself." Freddie said.

"What, are you nuts? Do you think going far will help you to put your act together? No Sir…ry! Why don't find yourself right here? You have the time to meditate all day long, here and now… or read whatever books you want. Why escape? You know your soul is within you… no matter where you are or where you go. So, think positive Please." I scolded him.

"Fine, I will stay here and suffer from all the pain… physical and non-physical, and wait for it to transform me into enlightenment. I will be the new Buddha… How about that?"

"That's sound great to me, but don't expect me to worship you… or become one of your followers, OK?" I said it amusingly, but poor Freddie could not laugh from the pain in his chest.

I later suggested that he should eat something. He agreed to eat some soup and toast. I convinced him to add some fruit salad and a cheesecake. I placed the order for him with room service and asked them to bring a bed tray. Then I left to have dinner with Melody at home.

Half an hour later and while Freddie was trying to eat his light dinner, his phone rang and it was Anne. That cheered him up and answered,

"Hi… thanks for calling. Sorry I couldn't call you earlier."

"How do you feel? Barry briefed me on what happened, you're resting now?"

"Yes, I am. I have to wait it out until the pain dissipates. The pills they gave me help, but I am still limited in my mobility." Freddie said.

"Were you scared when they picked you up?" Anne asked.

"Honestly… Yes! They were two rugged men who said they're doing this to punish me for not responding to their money order."

"What are you doing now?"

"I'm just trying to swallow some soup and toast. I didn't eat anything the last 24 hours. Barry has been a great help, he came to see me and ordered the food for me and he just left… I am so grateful for his friendship. How about you?"

"Been busy as expected. I saw 10 patients today and I just got home. You were in my mind all day. I'm sorry I'm not next to you to ease your pain." Anne passionately said.

"That's so sweet of you to say… thank you. I wish I could hug the pillow and pretend it's you; I can't even do that yet! By the way, I'm planning to use this bedtime to read and write… I can use the food tray to do that. Do you have any books you recommend that I should read?" Freddie asked.

"Let me think about it and I'll order a couple from Amazon to deliver to your suite by tomorrow. Writing is a good idea too. Don't keep your thoughts in, put them down on paper… or type them on your laptop if you can. Writing helps you to understand yourself better." Anne asked.

"Good guidance, thanks… by the way I miss looking at you, can we flip this to Facetime?"

"Oh no not now, I look awful and tired. Will try it later…"

"Come on! I've seen you without makeup and you look great either way! I am bruised and unshaved yet… I'm willing to show you the other side of me too. I also want a tour of your place to—to visualize you in your own home." Freddie demanded. There was silence for few seconds and then suddenly her face appeared on the screen. Freddie did the same and they both waved in harmony.

"You feel better now?" Anne asked.

"Yes of course, thanks and you look lovely… this is how I look now, what do you think? You can easily move! so please show me your place."

Anne moved around the apartment and showed Freddie the living room, the kitchen and dining area then, she showed him the bedroom and bathroom.

"This is it, satisfied now?"

"It is so cute and well decorated… Dr. Stevenson. Thank you, now I can visualize you walking around, and it's a good picture for my mind." Freddie said.

"How romantic, I sensed that about you. It goes well with your character. Tell me what do you plan to write about? A happy story, I hope? Even if it's not happy one, write it down and get it out of your system." Anne repeated.

"I don't know what I'm going to write about yet… but it'll come to me!"

"OK Freddie, I am hungry now Please excuse me, eat your desert and will talk later… Rest well and keep your chins up! I give you a big hug!" Anne said.

"Thanks again, a big hug and a kiss too…" Freddie said before they hung up.

CHAPTER 6

Court Hearings and New Surprises

Freddie was spending the rest of the week resting in his suite. I visited him for an hour every day and I brought some magazines and food to eat, knowing he was not eating well. Melody came with me twice and brought him flowers, which he appreciated.

The police detectives in Manhattan arraigned Jane and asked her to go with them to the office for further interrogation. They had her listen to her own voice on the two recorded phone conversations. They told her that the conman Marco Donneti who is now detained by the police in Queens had confessed, and he's behind bars now. She denied any involvement in the kidnapping of Freddie and asked to speak to her lawyer.

Jane's lawyer came while she was still at the police precinct. He was the same lawyer who pressed charges against Freddie and claimed a $2 M compensation for leaving Jane. He was shown the evidence the police had on her, and the lawyer advised her to cooperate. He said he'd be present for the quick court hearing already arranged by James the next day. Meanwhile she remained in the custody of the police until then.

James Atwood, and another junior partner from the firm were present at the hearing, along with Jane's lawyer, introduced as Harry Padowski. Judge Lumen presided and James, a well known litigator and prosecutor briefed the Judge about the case and reminded the court that Jane Neiman was the same person who claimed compensation in a previous case that was dismissed by the court.

James told the court,

"Your honor, Miss Jane Neiman plotted the kidnapping of Freddie Rodman, and she's the one who hired the kidnappers to cause the severe physical and emotional harm on Mr. Rodman, who's unable to be with us today as ordered by his doctors.

"Additionally, your Honor, we have two recordings, one of her conversation with the kidnapper, Mr. Marco Donneti, who is now behind bars in Queens… and who confessed that Ms. Neiman is the one who hired him to call Mr. Rodman and threatened to hurt him if he did not give him $2 million within 24 hours. And he is the one who performed the kidnapping and beating of Mr. Rodman. We have his affidavit as evidence.

"We also have another recording between Ms. Neiman and another man, unidentified, referring to some action, and we ask for your permission to question Ms. Neiman to reveal the identity of this gentleman. Thank you".

Judge Lumen then asked Mr. Padowski, Jane's defense lawyer, for his statement. He stood up and told the Judge,

"Your Honor, we have nothing to add." The lawyer said and sat down. Jane looked at him shocked and angry that he had nothing to say in her defense. Upon the request of James Atwood, the Judge asked Jane to come to the chair assigned for questioning. She took the chair and had to swear that 'she will speak the truth and nothing but the truth so help me God'. She looked nervous and pale in the face. She realized that she better tell the truth. James started to question her,

"Can you please state your full name and your exact home address."

"Jane Neiman… and I live in Manhattan New York at 521 gramercy street, apartment 105."

"Do you know Mr. Frederic Rodman personally?

"Yes, he was my boyfriend for almost one year."

"Was it you who sued him asking for $2 million after he broke up with you, and the court dismissed the case?"

"Yes!"

"Was it you, Ms. Neiman who hired Mr. Marco Donneti… to call Mr. Rodman and ask for $2 million to be delivered within 24 hours?" James asked.

"Yes!"

"Would you agree that it was also you… who instructed Mr. Donneti to kidnap and harm Mr. Rodman because he did not answer the two phone calls that Mr. Donneti made last Tuesday?"

"Yes, I agree." Jane replied.

"Are you aware of the extent of emotional and physical harm inflicted on Mr. Rodman, and how he was thrown out of the van in front of the hospital, after being beaten badly with a baseball bat that fractured and broke some of his chest ribs?" James asked aggressively.

"No I am not aware of the extent of his infliction." Jane said

"So you're not aware of his doctors orders not to move for at least one week, and he has to take sedatives… and painkillers in the interim?" James kept prodding her.

"No, I'm not aware… I'm sorry it went that far!" Jane admitted.

I have one final question Ms. Neiman. He pulled out a small recorder from his pocket and played the short conversation that Jane had with a certain male and asked her,

"Do you confirm first this was your voice?"

"Yes it is."

"Thank you… can you please identify whose voice it was of the person you spoke with?" James asked.

Jane went silent for few seconds and was very angry about her lawyers' attitude who threw her in the lions' pit to keep himself out of the loop. She then spoke and said,

"The person I was talking with is…um… Mr. Harry Padowski, who is sitting here with us in this court." She said, and pointed at her lawyer who's sitting at the defense table. The noise in the room got louder with chatter. Mr. Padowski sat there calmly, with a vicious smile on his face. Then James asked,

"You mean your own lawyer Mr. Padowski… was involved with you in the plot to coerce/embezzle and hurt Mr. Rodman?"

"Yes!"

"Was he the only one involved or there were others too?" James asked.

"I don't know who else, I know he has partners… but he was the one who dealt with me." Jane said nervously.

"Were you supposed um… to divide the money with him if you had succeeded to get it?"

"Yes, 70% to him and his partners, and 30% to me. I was a fool to play that game, but I also was threatened and forced to do it… or else I would be hurt too."

"Thank you Ms. Neiman for your excellent cooperation. Your honor, I have no further questions to Ms. Neiman, but… I would like to ask Mr. Padowski to take the chair for few questions if I may." James asked gleefully knowing that he won already.

"By all means Mr. Atwood. Mr. Padowski would you please come to the witness chair." The judge ordered.

Harry Padowski stood up and said,

"Your honor, I prefer not to do that, and I reserve my right to take the fifth."

"In that case Mr. Padowski, I hold you in contempt of Court and you will be detained. There will be a scheduled a court hearing… and be prepared to defend yourself or hire a lawyer." The Judge said, and ordered the plaintiff to handcuff Mr. Padowski and take him to the detention room inside. Then the judge continued,

"As for you Ms. Neiman, I will consider your testimony and I will revert with my decision tomorrow at 10:00 am… You have the right to appoint another lawyer, or just accept my sentence."

***

James called Freddie and told him he's on his way to see him. He has good news.

Freddie notified the front desk and asked that someone should accompany his guest to open the door. James later walked in with an employee from downstairs, pulled a chair and sat next to him. He expressed his wishes for a quick recovery then started,

"It went well today. Jane was fully cooperative and she confessed her involvement from the beginning, admitting that she hired the kidnapper, her conversation with him and she apologized for the pain she caused you. More interesting… when I asked her in court to identify the man in the second recorded phone conversation… she pointed at her lawyer Harry Padowski and said it was him… who pushed her to do the work in every step of the way.

"The Judge allowed me to question him but he refused and took the fifth. The judge then detained him until he asks for a court hearing; otherwise he's guilty too… So they are both behind bars, and Jane has to appear in the court again tomorrow morning to receive the Judge's sentence." James narrated.

"Wow, James! Is it all behind us now?" Freddie asked.

"As far as you are concerned yes… no one will bother you anymore. But we're not done yet with her lawyer, and his partners. And, we don't know what sentence Jane will receive tomorrow." James cheerfully said.

"Well done, thanks! We are now, with Matilda's case? Freddie asked.

"I have another meeting with her lawyer tomorrow… and will be able to let you know shortly thereafter."

"Thanks again James, will talk soon."

I called Freddie, who told me James had just left, and he gave me the good news in details. I told him to keep thinking positive, and to trust the Universe for future developments. He asked me to thank Simon and ask him to send the bill.

***

Freddie had the rest of the day to himself. He called the office and was satisfied that all was in order. It was too early to speak with Anne. He closed his eyes and tried to meditate. He realized that he was still unable to quiet his mind. All kinds of ideas were racing at high speed. He opened his eyes and decided to contemplate the recent development of his life. He wanted to start a journal to jot down his thoughts and the meaningful event of his day but was not yet comfortable to type or even write. He thought,

> "I am grateful that I am alive. I have two good friends in Barry and Anne that help to get over my inner and outer conflicts. They are straightforward with me, and encourage me to be strong and think positive. I am now going through a new experience for the first time in my life. I was kidnapped and beaten up. I am tolerating excruciating pain. I am trying to hold back my anger and temptation for revenge. I am realizing that there is an inner voice within me that I should

connect with. I have to learn to be more trusting despite the humiliation I went through. I believe I paid my price already. I need to target for a better future ahead.

"My good friend Barry is my only stable sounding board and I owe him my loyalty forever. My new friend Anne is a distant and enigmatic woman that I would like to know better. My settlement agreement with Matilda is almost finished and my relationship with my boys is improving. The Jane era and the consequences of that relationship are not to be forgotten and many lessons are to be learned here.

"Despite the recent solutions to many serious issues of the past, I still feel angst and anger within me. Should I just to go to the Fellowship in town, or seek shelter away from here to achieve my self-realization? Or is Barry right that going away is not the solution, as my soul is always within me, regardless to the location I am in? I am entitled to be happy and to live in peace. It is my birthright and I'll do whatever I can to get there."

Freddie found himself falling asleep after going through these thoughts. He closed his eyes and woke up an hour later. It was 7pm. He ordered some food as his appetite was getting better. He then called Anne for his evening conversation that he looked forward to. Anne answered the call and right away told him that she can't talk, and if he could please call her back in one hour.

Freddie spent his waiting time slowly eating his pasta and salad and did not touch his dessert, the cheesecake he likes, and decided to devour it later in the evening. He watched some news on TV and was interrupted by the ring of his phone. It was Anne. He turned the TV off and greeted her. She said,

"I am sorry Freddie I couldn't talk to you earlier. I had an unexpected visit from my annoying ex-husband who just dropped in. He left now, thank God!"

"Is everything alright? I—I thought you said you were divorced two years ago, are you… you still friends or something?" Freddie asked somewhat shocked.

"No, we're not friends at all. I broke up with him because I could not tolerate his obsessive/possessive and jealous character. He also wanted children, and I didn't… so it was painful, and I left him." Anne stated.

"Hum…mm, I never thought you had a rough period in your life. I consider you a perfect person." Freddie said.

"Now, wait a minute! who says I'm perfect? I may be a happy person, but not perfect! I have issues too. The fact that I'm in the business of helping people in their personal life does not mean I—I am immune from having personal problems myself. I am a normal human being after all." Anne clearly explained.

"I see! I appreciate your honest statement. I was about to build a statue for you, and bow in your presence daily, but I—I won't anymore. Come on Anne, don't underestimate who you are! This can't be true… you're an angel with no faults." Freddie said jokingly.

"Oh Freddie, get serious! I could tell you stories about me that can make you run a long distance away from me." Anne responded.

"I'm already a long distance away from you, how much farther can I go? So, feel free and tell me more about you… you are safe with me, and I will keep all your secrets to myself." Freddie said in his continued jolly mood.

"I love it when you talk silly, never mind! I like you and I trust you, so here we go. Secret no.1… I don't believe that sex and romance go together necessarily. I enjoy sex um… for the physical pleasure of it, and it doesn't have to be done to induce romance with the person I am enjoying it with. For me, sex is not a pre-requisite to falling in love with someone. I agree… I have to like, or be physically attracted to, the person I choose to have sex with, but not necessarily in love with, or hope to fall in love with, after sex. Am I making myself clear?" Anne explained.

"Are you saying as an example… what we had together, was just for physical pleasure, and once it was done it is gone… pufff…? Or, is it wrong to assume that the good feelings that remain alive after the sex should not trigger a special spark that could bring two people closer together? Freddie questioned Anne's explanation.

"In a way yes! Enjoying physical pleasure with someone does not necessarily mean that you will equally enjoy every other aspect of his or her character. One could be great in bed, but unbearable outside the bed.

If the person is great all around, which is rare, then go for it… and see how long it lasts?" Anne said.

"Perhaps you are talking about your past experience, and I tend to agree with you. The mistake I did um… was to allow sex to hook me into a new relationship, which turned out to be awful. And that was at the expense of losing a stable marriage, despite the fading sex aspect of it. I—I lost out in both cases. Why? Because I did not know what true love is… You remember our conversation about this subject?" Freddie referred about his ex relationships with both his wife and his girl friend, both lost.

"I fully understand what you're saying, and these mistakes happen in life… What I'm really saying, though is that I also could be satisfied with having just sex with people I like, as I did with you, without being in love first… The truth is that I don't believe I—I need to be in love with someone, in order for me to feel more complete or happier. In fact, I am not truly interested to be in a love relationship right now, I am happy with what I have." Anne spelled it out.

"I hear you loud and clear Anne, and it's good for me to know that now… and not to dream or expect what may not happen between us." Freddie said seriously.

"Freddie, please understand one thing, though I find you a great loving and warm person, you have um… other priorities in your life to focus on. You said that yourself… You're working on finding out who you are and what is it that you want out of your life that can make you happy. This is a wonderful future task, and I'm sure you will succeed. You and I can be great friends despite the distance between us. I'm fine, and you're fine. If we can be together again… I would love that! But, don't make me your priority in your life now, you'll be more confused." Anne calmly explained.

"Again, I thank you for making your position clear. I respect that… But tell me please, how do you satisfy your physical pleasures without having a husband or a boyfriend?" Freddie asked curiously.

"A good question! Between us as good friends, this is secret no. 2, when I feel like wanting pleasure, I—I either please myself alone or um… on occasions I do it with my friend, the girl I told you about… We both get pleasure out of being together, and neither one of us is in a relationship and, we are not lesbian. In fact, she is on the lookout for a male companion, though I'm not." Anne answered truthfully.

"I understand! So when it comes to physical pleasure... the gender to you is secondary. Am I right?" Freddie asked.

"Yes, you can say that. In fact I have no time to commit to a relationship with a man at this stage in my life. I am focusing on my career." Anne said.

"Anne! You're still an outstanding person to me and I love having a forthright conversation with you. I thank you for sharing your amazing outlook on life... and I will call you soon to see how you're doing." Freddie said.

"Wait... before you go? How do you feel now? Do you still have pain and anything new on the legal front?" Anne asked.

"Thanks for asking, I feel slightly better and I have less physical pain. I won the case against Jane... and her lawyer handler. I'm still emotionally shocked about the kidnapping but they are both behind bars now, awaiting the sentencing by the judge tomorrow. So a big brick is off my shoulder." Freddie explained.

"Very happy to hear that my friend... and please keep me advised."

***

Freddie sat back on his bed looking at the ceiling again reflecting on the conversation he just had with Anne. The big lesson he learnt is that life is always full of new twists and turns. He felt he has to bother me and tell me the story. So he called me,

"Hi, am I disturbing you?"

"No! go ahead Freddie, what's up?" I asked.

"I just hung up the phone with Anne... and guess what?"

"What? Did you make her pregnant... What? I asked.

"She does not believe that having sex with me um... means that she loves me, or wants to have a relationship with me?" Freddie said sadly.

"What else did you expect, you fool? Did you expect every one to be a softy like you? She's smart, she's wise... she knows the difference between love and having sex." I reacted.

"Gee! you sound like her... so I am a fool for love, right? Freddie complained.

"You said it! Did you not learn anything from the ugly and horrible relationship you had with Jane? Jane tricked you and sucked your blood when she sensed your weakness... and you fell for it right away... But this gorgeous woman Anne is just the opposite. She's honest and tells it as it is. Learn from her how to love yourself first, and think with your head, not with your mushy heart." I said..

"You know every time I call you I expect you to be loving, compassionate and considerate towards me. Instead you start scolding me and hammering me hard. Is this what good friends are for?" Freddie complained.

"You bet! This is why you engaged my services and hired me for free, as your alter ego… to be straightforward and truthful with you. You don't need me as a shoulder to cry on… You're not a kid anymore, grow up and look after yourself. Go do this… this self-realization thing you talked about. I—I respect Anne for being straight with you, and you…you should respect me for being direct as well. You're lucky to have us both as your friends. Anne's conversation with you-- like mine now-- *is* the foundation of true love. We don't ask for anything in return. We just care about you!" I strongly spilled my heart out.

"I love you man! You are right … I will spend the night pondering these great thoughts and I give you a big hug. Melody is lucky to have you! Good night."

***

Freddie had an hour before he went to sleep and was grateful to both conversations with Barry and Anne. He felt a special vibration of compassion that they both touched him with. He said to himself,

> *I want to embrace the Truth. It is a wonderful virtue. I understand why both of them live a happier life. I want to transform my own life to have peace happiness and lasting love. I realize that to change my current state of being I have to change my thoughts. That means to live a life without fear, without conflict, without clashes with other people, and to live a life with positive thoughts and good feelings.*
>
> *The challenge is to figure out how to go about it? No one else can do it for me. I have to get rid of my guilt feelings, to start enjoying living alone, to focus on my true self and connect with my Higher Self. I am determined not to give up on meditation and to keep searching within, to listen to my*

Inner Voice. I will keep attending the Fellowship meetings as soon as I can move around comfortably. No more suffering, the time is ripe to experience enlightenment."

Freddie felt much better spiritually. He enjoyed this new experience of analyzing his thoughts, and learned how to overcome his emotional disappointment about Anne. He was determined to practice self-love first, and the rest was secondary. He took a painkiller and went to sleep.

CHAPTER 7

Court Orders and a New Beginning

James went to the court the next morning to hear the Judge's decision regarding Jane. As they all stood up when Judge Lumen walked into the courtroom, James stared at Jane on the other side. She looked desolate and pretty nervous about her sentence. When every one was seated, the judge opened his file and read from a sheet of paper,

"Ms. Jane Neiman could you please stand."

Jane stood up and she was without a lawyer sitting next to her at the table. The Judge then continued:

"I noticed that you are not being represented today by your counsel… that's fine. I deliberated deeply about your case and I hold you equally responsible for implementing the wrong request for compensation and the eventual harm you caused to Mr. Fredric Rodman. The judge who handled the hearing for Mr. Donneti in Queens, called me and told me that he sentenced him with a 5-year imprisonment plus $200,000 fine to be paid to Mr. Rodman.

"As it regards your role, and as it was revealed yesterday that you were acting on behalf of, or coerced by another group, and you executed orders from Mr. Harry Padowski; and given that you cooperated in revealing the truth, I reduced your sentence to three years in jail and a fine of $300,000 to be paid to Mr. Rodman and I leave it at his discretion. As you may know, you also have the right to appeal my sentence to a higher court."

Jane had her head looking down and started sobbing upon hearing the sentence. She asked for permission to speak. Judge Lumen nodded and she said,

"Your Honor, I will not appeal your sentence, as I do not wish to have lawyers representing me anymore. You saw how they all lied to me and disappeared. However, I do not have the money you are asking me to pay. Can you be more merciful with me Please?"

"The amount of money can be discussed with Mr. Rodman's attorneys and I give them the discretion to decide the amount they want you to pay. Now, you will be escorted to serve your term at the designated jail. Is that all?" Judge Lumen said.

"Your Honor what happens to Mr. Padowski and his partners who put me in this hole?" Jane asked.

"That is another case Ms. Neiman and it will be handled promptly and diligently. I believe Mr. Atwood, has already requested a court hearing tomorrow in this regard." Judge Lumen replied.

"Thank you your Honor!" Jane said before she was handcuffed and escorted outside the room and continued her sobbing.

Meanwhile Judge Lumen asked James to approach the bench. He told him that Mr. Padowski will represent himself and the court hearing will be at 9:30 am the next day. James agreed and got permission to leave the court. When he walked outside, he called Freddie and gave him the news about Jane's sentence and the court hearing the next day. He asked Freddie to think about the money from Jane. Freddie reminded James to finish the settlement with Matilda.

***

Freddie informed me about the court orders and Jane's sentence. He asked me if I should be merciful with the fine amount. I said,

"Freddie it is your call… given that she admitted her mistakes and the real villains were her sponsors, I would reduce the amount to the extent she can afford, and ask her to pay it directly to a charity of her choice."

"That's what I wanted to hear. Thanks! Tomorrow is the hearing of her lawyer, who's going to defend himself. James filed the complaint and will see how it goes. In his case, um I expect the sentence to be more severe."

"Any news on the settlement agreement?" I asked.

"Almost done, not fully finalized yet but close! Meanwhile, I am having second thoughts about Anne. I will stay good friends with her, but

I can't hope for more. As we talked last time, I will focus on loving myself and leave the rest to the Universe." Freddie said.

"Good decision! You should not be hurt by her—her honest truth. Besides, if you step back and take a break, while you work on your own situation, you'll see how the universe might introduce you to meet another person. Who knows? I assure you that… with your revised magnetic personality, you will attract a host of candidates for you to choose from. When Anne finds out, I bet you she'll run back to your arms. Think highly of yourself Freddie!" I explained sympathetically.

"Well said, please tell Melody to wait a while, before she introduces me to her friend, I am not in a hurry at any rate. I need to go through this painful period before I am can be revised as you said." Freddie responded confidently.

"Okay, I will. By the way I met this lady she's stunning! I'm sure you'll like her." I said teasingly.

"I'm available next week… if you like!" Freddie rushed to say.

"You see… I told you! You can't be without a woman for a long time." I reacted immediately.

"I'm kidding Barry… just save her till later. I'm serious about focusing on me for now." Freddie seriously stated.

"Wise decision! I will see you later. Enjoy the rest of your day."

***

In the middle of the afternoon the concierge called Freddie and told him that he received a small package and if they can bring it over to his room. within five minutes the door opened and it was a package of books from Amazon. He remembered that Anne had promised to send them to him. There were three books inside the small box. The titles of the books:

1. *Self Realization for Regular People*, by Anastasia Netri
2. *Get Out of Your Mind & Into Your Life*, by Steven Hayes
3. *Unconditional Love*, by Kelly Elliot.

Freddie was happy to receive the books and he read the reviews on the back covers. Anne chose the right subjects as per their earlier discussions.

As Anne was still at work, he decided to send her a 'thank you' message instead of calling her. He figured he should start reading book no. 1, which was written for 'regular people like him'. He first read the note from the author and noted part of what it said:

Quote
- *Why self-realization is NOT one-size-fits-all*
- *Redefining love (yup, I go there!)*
- *Why the things that piss you off are pointing you directly to your liberation*
- *When Truth becomes more real than the lie*
- *The "transformation spiral" - truth bomb: you're never "done".*

I really do believe that this is your moment to awaken
Unquote

Freddie liked the little he read. It looked like material directed straight at him. He became eager to read the book in its entirety.

He continued reading the book and could not put it down. He appreciated the blunt style of the author and the fact that there were no 'sugarcoating' statements. It was truly meant to awaken 'the hibernating bear 'within me' and pushing me to search for my 'own journey to *MY* Truth'. (I called and interrupted his reading and said I'm on my way over.)

I walked in and saw Freddie immersed in a book and taking notes. Freddie did not even look at me when I said 'hi'. I sat down wondering what's going in with him. He remained silent for a while until he finished a paragraph he was reading. Then he spoke,

"Hi again, I'm sorry… I just wanted to finish this paragraph of this amazing book that Anne sent me. How are you?"

"I'm fine, is this a bad time? I can come later when you're with your normal self." I said to him with a wondering look?

"No…no… sit please, sit." He replied.

"Good, a follower of Anne now! I'm proud of you, what's the book about?" I asked.

"About Self-Realization!" He looked at me and said it emphatically.

"Are you self-realized yet?" I asked jokingly.

"You bet! Keep making fun of me… it makes you feel better! Are you here to pick on me now? Go ahead… keep going!" Freddie said agitated.

"OK, enough already! What else did she send you? Books on Romance?" I couldn't stop being ridiculous.

"Well let me see here… what's in the box… two erotic books and one porn video? Do you want to watch it with me?" Freddie seemed uptight saying it.

"OK… I think I went too far. I just wanted to cheer you up with my silly jokes… silly man! So tell me, what's the latest?" I asked.

"I don't know, ask me tomorrow after the court hearing. James said he'd call me right away. I expect justice to be done finally." Freddie opinionated.

"Are you feeling better, with less pain now?"

"I guess! I tolerate it better, couple more days and it'll be over I hope? I am anxious to start moving around already. Anyhow these books arrived on time. I'll nourish my soul in the interim!" Freddie said gladly.

"Did Anne respond to your 'thank you' message?"

"No, not yet!"

"Do you miss her?"

"No! Not lately… after our last conversation, I'm cool about the whole thing. I consider her a good friend now, that's all." Freddie said to save face. He was not really sure he fully meant what he said.

"I'm pleased to hear that. I was afraid she might replace me as your best friend." I said half-seriously.

"Don't worry your place in my heart is cast in stone… no one can replace you, sweet pumpkin!"

"Oh! I like to be called pumpkin. Is this going to be my new nickname now?" I responded facetiously.

"Yes, until I meet another Anne. I have to spoil someone, and it's your turn now, happy?" Freddie joked.

"Very! Take your time… take a whole year or so. It's such an honor to be spoiled by you." I reacted equally.

"Are you going to eat with me, or is Melody cooking something for you?" Freddie asked. I looked at my watch and said,

"I have to go in 5 minutes. Yes, she's cooking a special meal for me… eat your heart out! Do you want me to order some food for you?" I asked.

"Yes please, a large rib-eye steak, a big plate of spaghetti, a huge mixed salad, a double cheesecake and… a bottle of red wine." Freddie said.

I called room service and placed an order for a small portion of spaghetti vongole, a glass of wine and a slice of cheesecake. Freddie looked at me and wanted to throw a book at me because I did not execute his initial order. I jumped up and said goodbye.

Freddie ate and spent the rest of the evening reading his new book.

***

He slept better that night, though he spent a good part of his sleep visualizing the process towards self-realization. He imagined scenes where he was in the company of angels that were redefining the concept of love for him, and showing him how he can stop living a lie. He went to sleep with the knowledge that he is the only one that can reach the end of his journey. There was no one rule that fits all, every individual journey is unique and it may be a long curvy road as well.

***

He ordered coffee and toast from room service when he woke up to a new day. He immediately delved into the reading of the book. He was ready to start the chapter about the Law of Attraction when his phone rang. He looked at his watch and noticed it was 11:35 am. It was James on the phone. He said,

"I'm still at the courthouse, outside. Things went well though. Harry Padowski didn't do a good job defending his own case. He stuck to the fact that he was the only one who advised Jane to execute his orders step by step.

"He denied that there was a club that includes other people… or, a physical organization that controls these operations. He insisted that apart from Jane, he was the only person involved… At this moment, we don't know if he—he is telling the truth, or taking the full responsibility alone, in order to protect the position of his other colleagues?" James said.

"What will happen next, James?"

"The Judge gave us one hour recess, and we return at 12:30 pm to resume. I told him I'm not done interrogating the defendant."

"Why you're not done, James?" Freddie asked.

"I'm using this time for two reasons: one, I'm sending one of my colleagues to see Jane, and ask her again if she knew of other people involved. And two, my firm is doing thorough investigation about the firm where Padowski works, to see if we can dig something odd about them." James said.

"Well done! Let me know what happens and thanks."

***

Freddie went back to his book and read about the Law of Attraction. He researched online to understand what it really means. He learned that it is the most important Universal Law that has been spread widely in recent years. It's a philosophy derived from the school of New Thought. He read that quantum physics embellished the idea that the Universe consists of pure forms of energy, and we humans are part of it. The Law of Attraction emphasized the fact that positive thoughts and feelings attract positive experiences. 'Like attracts Like'. To change our negative thoughts and feelings we could visualize that the desired positive states of being have already occurred.

Freddie remembered how the movie and the book, "the Secret" popularized the law of attraction around the world. It did not resonate with him well at that time in 2006. However the book he was reading now was more meaningful to him, as it coincided with his own search to achieve self-realization.

While he was reflecting on these new thoughts and suggestions his mobile phone rang. It was Anne.

"Hi Anne, how are you? I am half way through the book you sent me on 'self-realization for regular people'… thanks a lot, I love it. Thank you also for the other two books, I'm sure they are good too."

"Great! I'm glad you're enjoying reading them, how do you feel?"

"Better! Thanks, the pain is diminishing, and I—I am sleeping better. Still busy with work?" Freddie asked.

"Yup! Busy as usual. I just got home an hour ago, had something to eat and here I am talking to my handsome New York friend." Anne responded.

"Anne, do you believe in the Law of Attraction?" Freddie was curious to find out from her.

"Of course I do! Some researchers don't. They think it is a pseudoscience … or misusing scientific concepts. I believe, like many others, that the law of attraction is always in operation, whether we are tuned in to it or not. It doesn't rest or sleep, and we all experience and actualize what we mostly think about, what we desire, or expect from our life be it good or bad." Anne explained.

"I agree! I look back and see that from my own experiences, particularly my personal relationships. Now I understand how I attracted what I was mostly thinking about… Whenever I thought negative I got a negative experience… And whenever I thought positive I got a positive experience. The law of attraction is impersonal, it gives us what we ask for, and be it negative or positive… Amazing!" Freddie felt good saying that.

"That's right Freddie, you are a fast learner. I had similar experiences in my life too, and now I can easily anticipate the outcome of thoughts that enter my mind before hand. That is why I always try to only think and feel positive, as I told you before. I tell you, it saves us many headaches." Anne said.

"Thanks Anne, I very much miss our conversations… and I'm so glad we are such good friends now. You are a very special woman indeed! Thanks again for the books. I will study them thoroughly, I promise." Freddie said.

"Before you go, what is the latest on your legal front?" Anne was curious to know.

"Jane was sentenced to three years in Jail and a fine of $300,000. Her lawyer, who was also… the one who plotted the whole deal, had his court hearing today and is expected to receive a heavier sentence tomorrow, according to my lawyer. Other than that, my settlement agreement with my ex is almost done." Freddie shared the truth with Anne.

"You see! Things are improving, despite the discomfort you had to go through… You are feeling better physically, you are more relaxed emotionally… and you are moving forward spiritually. That's great, don't you think?" Anne said, gladly.

"Thanks! A good part of that improvement is because you appeared in my life… Please don't disappear on me! You know how much I like you and appreciate your presence around, though you're not around physically." Freddie lamented with his last words.

"We struck a valuable relationship between us, Fredric. I will keep my part of it intact. I hope you do too." Anne said assuredly.

"I promise I will. I hold you in great esteem and hope we can be together soon. I miss that, and by the way… I like it when you call me Fredric!"

"Well it came out natural… perhaps because I see the child in you is finally growing up. And, Fredric is more masculine and sounds more sexy, don't you think? I leave you with these happy thoughts, and will talk soon. Good night!" Anne concluded.

"Good night to you too. Thanks for the call and the books."

Freddie felt good after the conversation with Anne, and wondered why James didn't call him back regarding the afternoon session. He called him.

"Hello, this is James!"

"Hey, you didn't call me back this afternoon. What happened?"

"I'm sorry I didn't call you because the Judge had to postpone the hearing till tomorrow… I should have told you. Anyhow my colleague met with Jane and she told him she's sure there were other people in the firm who were involved, the reason why they wanted 70%. She did not know who they were, or their names. I will also receive more info tonight on the research my people in the office are conducting on their firm… Rest well and will talk tomorrow." James said.

Freddie, or 'Fredric', continued reading the book and was trying to finish it before he goes to sleep.

***

Six days had passed since the incidence took place, and Freddie was feeling better and noticed he can move his shoulders and wait more comfortably. His chest was still sore but not as painful. He cut back on taking pills and was scheduled to see the doctor in two days.

He continued reading the same book and had a couple more chapters to finish it. He took more notes and kept telling himself how it's not easy to be self-actualized. Just before he finished closing the book around noon, his phone rang and it was his lawyer, James.

"Hello James, what's the latest." Freddie asked.

"A lot happened. We found out from the research we did… that the Padowski firm had other cases, whereby other lawyers were the handlers.

They coerced rich clients to pay up and settle out of fear. I interrogated Padowski, and he confirmed the name of his other two lawyers in the same firm. I showed the Judge the evidence we had on the other cases, and proved that the law firm was in fact acting as a 'club' that sponsored and pushed women like Jane... The judge was overwhelmed by these findings, and—and discretely authorized the FBI to invade their offices and confiscate all their files... and to arrest the other lawyers who worked at the firm for questioning, while in custody of the police." James took a breath to slow down his excitement before he continued to say,

"Judge Lumen decided to keep the Padowski case pending until the FBI goes through the files first, and report their findings to the judge. He gave them three days to report back." James concluded.

"Wow... Wow! I can't believe this. Lawyers acting as gangsters? What do you think will happen, James?" Freddie asked.

"I don't know yet... we need more proof that they conducted these criminal acts. All I know is that um ... if proven guilty the consequences are severe. Will know in three days. Meanwhile, the good news is that we finalized the negotiations of the settlement agreement with Matilda's lawyers. Do you care to know the details? They're quite similar to what I told you last." James explained.

"No, that's fine, prepare it and I'll sign any required document. Thanks." Freddie asked.

"OK, how about Jane's fine did you consider?" James asked.

"Please have another meeting and ask her what she can afford and let me know."

"Noted, Freddie, and I hope you're getting better."

"I am, thanks! and have a good day."

***

After lunch, Freddie started reading the next book, *"Get out of your mind, and into your life"* by Steven Hayes. From the reviews he rad about the book he noticed that the author is introducing a new psychotherapy referred to as ACT, or 'Acceptance and Commitment Therapy'. It shows a way out of suffering into doing what matters the most in anyone's daily life. Freddie understood why Anne, a psychotherapist herself, chose this book. It was quite fitting the situation that Freddie was in.

He kept reading this book until 6:30 pm. I walked in shortly thereafter and was pleased to see my friend Freddie in better mood and moving around outside the bed. He smiled when he saw me, a rare sight lately. He looked at me and said,

"I've become a bookworm these past few days… I'm into my second book now and watch out, I'll be teaching you how to live your life soon."

"Bravo! That'll be an honor, professor Fredric." I gladly said.

"Anne called me Fredric yesterday, I want you to know! She said she finds calling me 'Fredric' more masculine and sexy… How about that?" Freddie said childishly.

"Oouh! How sexy? That must have lifted your spirits and alleviated your chest pain!" I said lightly.

"Here we go again, no rest for the weary! Are you jealous or something? Should I not share these… intimate remarks with you again? The woman finds me sexy… period!" Freddie complained.

"OK fine! How are enjoying your books?" I asked.

"The books are amazing and timely. What I wanted to tell you is what happened at the court today. The Law Firm that represented Jane… turned out to be a bunch of crooks, and they were caught performing other similar cases like mine. The FBI raided their offices, and the three lawyers of the firm are all in custody of the police now." Freddie told me.

"Say what? This is unbelievable… Crooks?" I reacted strangely.

"My sentiments exactly! The FBI will report their findings to the judge in three days. Poor Jane! She's been coerced all this time. By the way I instructed my lawyers to tell her to pay what she can afford … directly to a charity of her choice." Freddie reported.

"That's honorable of you to be merciful. It's enough that she has to be living in a cage for three years." I said.

"By the way Barry, can you please call Matilda and tell her that I won't be in a position um … to see the kids this weekend." Freddie asked.

"I did that already, yesterday!" I said.

"How? Why?"

"Because she called me to ask about you, and to thank you for finishing the settlement agreement without further arguments. What a benevolent man! You're my hero!" I said.

"Hey… one has to move on in life! I really seek a change from here on. I am getting better on all fronts. I still have to get over my guilt feelings… about leaving the kids, but I'm certain this will be resolved soon." Freddie responded positively.

"Good riddance! You will, and I bet you the communication with Matilda will improve from now on." I reassured him.

I left Freddie in a good mood that day and we agreed to meet again during the weekend.

He spent the rest of the week reading and taking notes and preparing to see the doctor again next week.

CHAPTER 8

A Legal Blowout

Freddie retuned from the hospital check-up with a clean bill of health. He was told to move around slowly and not to carry heavy loads. James called him shortly thereafter. He said the FBI submitted their report to Judge Lumen. They found that the law firm was heavily involved in a network of sponsoring and training several women to do exactly what Jane did.

The story goes where beautiful young women hunt and hook up with rich older men, in bars or social parties. They lure them to bed, and then create unhappy environments for them weeks later. They were coached to slowly start disagreements and arguments with the men, their 'clients', so to speak, and demand financial increases, until these men get fed up and breakup with them. And if the men decide to walk away, they get sued shortly thereafter.

Freddie asked him,

"How many such cases were similar to mine?"

"Yours was only one of three cases that involved violence… The men in those cases succumbed to their demands and paid. Other men in other cases settled and paid out of fear of being embarrassed in public… or caught by their wives. This had been going on for the last three years. There were several millions collected as such. The files had names of all the women and a list… of the hit men who did the dirty work."

"What will happen to these lawyers now?" Freddie was curious to know.

"Judge Lumen had all the evidence he needed to convict them, but decided to—to postpone the sentencing till tomorrow at 10:00 am. I doubt his sentence will be lenient… He was quite amazed by the evidence he saw.

Will see what happens tomorrow! I'll let you know." James said before he ended the call.

Meanwhile, Freddie saw on TV that the news of the court hearing leaked out to the media. He was certain that a host of reporters and cameramen would crowd the court the next day.

***

And so it was. The courtroom was filled with people. Cameramen and photos were not allowed inside. Many reporters attended nevertheless. The room was buzzing with noise and chatter. The three lawyers were seated at one desk and James with his colleague on the other side. Judge Lumen was announced and every body rose until he ordered people to sit. He looked at the crowd, and started with a small speech,

"I see we have a full room this morning! I expect you all to be quiet. The purpose of this session is to impose my sentence on the defendants whom I now ask to stand.

"I have been a judge for 15 years, and a lawyer the previous 20 years. With the all experience I've had, and the cases I heard, I never came across a case like this one. I've seen lawyers, and sometimes judges, make mistakes. But to see seasoned lawyers perform such heinous acts, even worse than the underground 'mafia-type' stories we hear, is beyond my comprehension.

"Last night I contemplated your deeds and went through the evidence delivered to me by the FBI. I was astounded, aghast, thunderstruck, and horrified, to say the least. I am amazed by the audacity of your acts, and your shameless continuation of the same crime during the past three years.

"As a previous lawyer myself, I am ashamed of what you have done. Our entire community is ashamed of what you have done too. Now, based on your confession to the crimes you committed, and the evidence supporting them, I formulated my sentence, without a jury, as you preferred.

"First, I sentence you Mr. Harry Padowski to 10 years in prison and a fine of $1 million to be paid to Mr. Rodman for masterminding the plot and hurting Mr. Fredric Rodman. As for the two you, Mr. Antony Camaro, and Mr. Joseph Lindman, you will serve 8 years in prison, and pay a fine of $1 million each, to be paid in part to the U.S. government and the rest for better monitoring by the Bar Association.

"Additionally, you are all disbarred from practicing law in the state of New York. Your bank accounts and assets will be frozen until the sentenced fines are paid in full within 45 days. All records show you have the money. And lastly your offices will be permanently shutdown.

"Furthermore, and upon your release from imprisonment, you will be placed on a supervised release for a period of two years, with full compliance to the rules and regulations of the U.S. Probation Office.

"You have the right to appoint a lawyer to appeal to a higher court… This session is adjourned." The courtroom was bursting with noise, and the cameramen ran through the big door to try and take photos of the three lawyers.

The three lawyers were handcuffed and taken outside the courtroom via a side door to be handed over to the police to take them to jail.

By the time James had a chance to call Freddie and report the decision by the Judge, Freddie heard about the sentence from the 'Breaking News' on major TV networks.

He later read the afternoon papers, which also referred to his case with Jane, which started the whole scandal. He was not happy about that. He wondered if his kids would get to hear about it directly or from other kids. Feelings of shame creped into his mind again and that polluted the flow of good thoughts he had enjoyed the past few days.

Bad news flies fast, and my colleagues at work brought me newspapers to read the past about my friend Freddie and the sentence the lawyers had received. I decided to wait to see his reaction when I see him later after work. The story was being discussed in many social circles, homes and offices around the country. It became a good gossip piece that entertained many, yet brought about controversial discussions in legal communities. Several people thought that the judge was lenient in his sentence while others thought he was too harsh. The main conclusion all agreed upon was the high level of greed that these lawyers were blinded by.

***

I saw Freddie after work as expected, and I found him in a pensive mood when I walked in.

"I'm happy to see you sitting in the living room for a change. You must be feeling better. When do you plan to go back to work?" I asked.

"I'll start tomorrow… I have to take it easy for a while longer though. What do you make out of the Court sentencing today?" Freddie asked me.

"The news is all over the place… I'm personally shocked how lawyers can have such a low caliber of morality and a high level of greed. The judge was more than fair in his sentencing. They deserve to be jailed for life if you ask me!" I stated.

"I've been thinking if there was something I could do as a result of this experience!" Freddie pondered.

"Like what?" I asked.

"I've been thinking! I want to create a non-profit organization, and call it Dignity Above All, or DAA, to guide, educate and empower young promising women to abstain from being coerced to perform similar acts." Freddie said.

"Wow, dear friend! This is a great idea. How do you plan to go about it." I asked again.

"I'll spearhead the project and hmm… deposit the money from the villains in the organization account. I'll check with James if Jane can be released from Jail sooner… and employ her to work at DAA, instead of her paying me back money. We are both notoriously famous now, so this should attract a lot of attention from women and men who seek dignified alternatives in their life." Freddie said seriously.

"I must tell you! I don't know what happened to you. Is it the incident, the books you're reading… your being alone for a while, or whatever? Man, you've changed so much in such a short while. And, um… I'm so proud of you. I would say go for it, and you're my hero!" I proudly said my piece.

"Thanks, this means a lot to me, coming from you! I will start to put the wheels in motion. How about you? Is all okay with you and Melody?" Freddie asked.

"Yeah… all is fine. I'm thinking about proposing to her soon. I'm not getting younger, and she's the perfect match for me, what do you think?" I said.

"This is great news buddy, I'm so happy to hear that… You waited long enough to meet the right person and now you have her. Just remember me when you think about the best man, you hear?" Freddie said joyfully.

"I don't know! I don't have anybody in mind, whom do you recommend?" I said jokingly.

"You're looking at him dear fellow! One of the best."

"You bet. I'll think about it." I responded facetiously. Freddie laughed and I joined him with a hug.

Freddie was eager to hear the latest news about the case and he switched on the TV. We came across a debate at one of the major networks consisting of an elite panel of 4 lawyers discussing the story and its impact on the moral legal system in the country. One prominent lawyer said,

"This recent uproar has yet to subside, and I'm glad it created so much noise in our field… I say, shame on these lawyers who blemished our honor, our respect and our commitment to the best legal system in the world. It's a pity Judge Lumen is not a federal judge, to disbar them across the nation."

Another panelist responded,

"I agree with you… and I believe the imprisonment sentence was too short. These guys belong in jail the rest of their lives. What they did is utterly disgusting."

The debate went on for another 20 minutes and the gist of it dwelled on the illness of greed and malice. One lawyer hoped that young women should be careful and someone should help them to be aware of such traps. Freddie sat up and told me,

"Did you hear that? I am going to be the one to teach women to be aware, as this guy said… Wow! I'm also going to advise men how to steer away from such temptations. I'm really inspired now." Freddie said enthused.

I invited Freddie to come and have dinner with us at home next Thursday. I told him Melody cooks a meatloaf not to forget. You'll be surprised.

***

James called Freddie and asked if he could come over and sign the settlement agreement. I seized this opportunity to discuss with him my idea for the new organization. As soon as I signed the agreement, James asked me,

"Aren't you going to read it first?"

"What for? I trust you guys and it's my family after all… Let them have what they want." Freddie replied.

"Great! What else do you have in mind? James asked.

I explained the idea of DAA I had, and asked James if he can register such an organization in New York; and he'll find the right location for it in Manhattan. Then he asked him to look into persuading the judge to release Jane form jail as soon as feasible, and explain the reason why. James found this idea very nonconventional, yet he said he would try. Just at the time James stood up to leave Freddie's phone rang. It was Anne. He told her to wait one second until he said goodbye to his lawyer. Then he answered. Before he spoke, Anne said,

"Your story is all over the news Fredric! You're a celebrity now… I'm impressed. Will you still recognize me?"

"Stop it Anne, how are you?"

"I'm fine… I just flipped the TV on and your photo was on the screen, and I froze! I heard the rest of the news and kept saying *wow* to myself. What a story? Lawyers… I mean lawyers doing this? What's happening to people in this affluent and greedy society of ours?" Anne said repulsively.

"I know! There are many lessons to be learned from this?" Freddie said.

"What did you learn, Fredric, enlighten me?" Anne asked curiously.

"I'm starting a non-profit organization um with the $1.2 million I'll receive from the villain lawyer who prompted Jane to do what she did, and the kidnapper who also hit me. It will be an active voice… to educate and train young pretty women to choose dignity over greed and malice and to learn something new for a career. The same to men. I'm thinking of calling it DAA, or 'Dignity Above All'. What do you think"

"Fredric, what an amazing idea and honorable act… I'm so proud of you my friend! I wish I—I could be there next to you now, to hug you. I congratulate you for this wonderful transformation you're going through. Tell me, what inspired you to--to come up with this idea? Anne asked anxiously.

"It's my Inner Voice, I guess! Thanks to you, and the books you sent me that opened my eyes and my heart to think along these lines. What amazes me is how—how the Universe functions in a mysterious way. It taught me how to turn negative events into positive opportunities … It is the enlightenment after the suffering, as you know, my dear spiritual advisor."

"Hey! You… you are my professor now. I will sit by your feet and learn from you, from now on… My student has bypassed me, and I am elated to see that happening in your life." Anne said happily.

"How about you? what's new in your life, other than the busy work?" Freddie asked.

"The only new good thing happening is that the girl friend I told you about, met a wonderful man and she's in love with him. They are planning to get married soon. So that's new!" Anne said.

"How are you taking it Anne? Given the close relationship you too have had?" Freddie asked in a friendly way.

"Pretty well I think, I'm happy for her. The relationship was good while it lasted. We'll still be friends. I'm open for new adventures now, I guess!" Anne explained.

"What kind of adventure Anne? Do you mean finding another lady friend, or… a man to fall in love with? Don't' you think it's time now?"

"I don't know yet, to tell you the truth! I'm not sure, um… if I'm ready to be with another man yet. Perhaps the terrible relationship I had with Mark, my ex, discourages me from a repeat performance. And honestly, the fun I had with my girl friend was not meaningful either, it was superficial. So, I don't know, you're my professor now, you tell me." Anne explained truthfully.

"Professor? Yes of course! Please don't underestimate yourself and remember how strong you are. Perhaps it's your turn to do some inner search, and I'm sure you know how to go about it my dear. You know what I think of you and how I feel about you… I want you to have the best life. So go do it!" Freddie said encouragingly.

"I love it when you talk to me like that Fredric… I mean it. No one has told this before to go in and check what's going on inside. Normally I'm the one who tells people what to do in this regard. Anyhow, look at you! you are a completely new person… again, I'm so impressed, and I love it!"

"I go to work tomorrow, and the concierge tells me to take the service elevator… because there are many reporters and cameramen have been waiting in the lobby waiting to interview me… Do you think I should face the music and tell them about my plan?" Freddie asked.

"It wouldn't hurt, you might as well seize this opportunity and express your opinion... while the iron is till hot. It may attract other donors to your organization in advance." Anne elaborated.

"You're right and you're so smart! I love that about you... Why don't you come and help me out with all this? No pressure, I'm only saying how great that would be." Freddie said.

"You'll never know, I may surprise you! It's been several weeks now since I saw you last... and I miss being with you." Anne said warmly.

"Wouldn't that be a treat? I'd love it if you ever get serious about it." Freddie beseeched.

"OK... will talk soon and good luck." Anne said.

***

Freddie got dressed to go to work and left his suite at 8:45 am, and took the elevator down. Three reporters and their cameramen were waiting for him when he walked out of the elevator. He stood in the main lobby and they circled him asking questions. He signaled to them with a stop sign and asked them to ask one a time.

One asked, "Was Justice done in your opinion, Sir?"

"We have an excellent justice system... and I am certain the Judge did a very good job."

Another question was asked,

"Are you satisfied with the $1.2 million fines you will receive?"

"Again I agree with the Judge's decision."

The same reporter followed with another question,

"What do you intend to do with all this money, Sir?"

"Hum-mm I decided to become an activist... advocating alternative ways for women to live a more dignified and skilled life... instead of pursuing the route of immorality and harassment coercing men to--to pay big unlawful amounts of money."

"How will you go about doing that?'" another reporter asked.

"I am starting a new non-profit organization called DAA, 'Dignity Above All' and I will deposit the first $1.2 million I receive from the sentence in its account... I will hire the right staff to--to locate and attract women to join and get trained with new skills... and help them find decent jobs in this wonderful city. We will offer them better alternatives than the immoral jobs you heard about. I will also figure out a program to advise men to remain loyal to their wives."

"How about the sentence that um… Jane Neiman, your ex girl friend received? Will she pay the half a million as well?" one of the reporters asked.

"The judge gave me um… the discretion to reduce the amount. Since she was coerced herself into the deal by her own lawyer, I intend to be more merciful, and ask her to work in the new organization pro bono instead of paying me back once she is released form Jail. She herself can be a great example to many who hopefully… would follow her advice. I don't know if she'll agree, but I asked my lawyer to discuss with her… and to ask the judge to reconsider her imprisonment time. Thank you all, I have to go to work." Freddie concluded the questioning and went on his way to the office.

Freddie arrived in his office at 9:00 am and saw the entire staff waiting for him in the lobby with a banner, and the words *'Welcome Back Boss'* written on it in large green letters. They all clapped and cheered when he walked out of the elevator. He shook hands with all of them and was very grateful to their good wishes.

Twenty minutes after he sat down behind his desk his assistant walked in and asked him to turn on the TV. He did and the questioning he just had with was already being broadcasted as breaking news, on a national channel. He remembered that we are now living in a high-tech digital age, where news moves at very fast speed. Fifteen minutes later the same assistant walked in saying the phone keeps ringing with calls from many publications and news channels asking for interviews. Freddie told her to take messages and he'll figure out what to do with it later. The news about his non-profit organization financed by his own money was like a bombshell that sent ripple effects across the land.

***

Freddie's assistant handed him 12 messages from different callers representing magazine, journals and TV stations. He told her to call them and say he'll call back the next day. He wanted to pick on my brains first to formulate the right answers. He called me and I told him I'd come to see him at 6:00 pm in his hotel.

I showed up on time and I greeted him saying,

"What an honor to visit with a celebrity? My.. oh.. My... you're the main story on TV... Soon you'll be asked to write your memoirs and make a movie about your life experiences. Happy?" I started.

"Good to see you too my mentor! I'm sure you saw the questioning this morning. Did I say too much?" Freddie responded.

"No... I thought it was good! You're not bad in front the camera. You should become a movie star. Serious! You speak well and you look very--very handsome. I'm jealous!" I joked.

"Here we go again! Listen I had 12 messages for interviews today, and I said will call back tomorrow. Do you have any advise?"

"Advise about what Freddie? I told you! You handled yourself well today."

"Not about that you smart elk? Should I um… agree to all interviews or choose a handful max?" Freddie asked.

"It depends how popular you want to be… and how much time and patience you have to--to repeat the same shenanigan every time." I said.

"Truthfully, I'm serious about becoming an activist… to help other women not to fall in the trap that—that Jane fell into, and the damage it caused me. My own story should also help other men to be more aware of what could happen if they cheat around, stuff like that. So, maybe I can take advantage of the current gossip stream… and promote my new organization. The more I talk about it the more people would know about its purpose and eventually contact the organization for advice… Am I crazy to think like that?" Freddie wondered.

"You're not crazy, you're an opportunist, a businessman… pick the top 5 or 6 most widely read papers, or magazines and… one TV channel, perhaps PBS, and see what you receive as response and go from there." I said and looked at my watch.

"I agree. I'll also do the interviews in my office… it's easier. Thanks for coming and I'll see you Thursday for dinner." Freddie said before his goodbye hug.

CHAPTER 9

Commitment to Change

Freddie reviewed the list of potential interviews the next day in his office. He chose to go with the local companies first: The New York Times and The New York Post daily newspapers; the New Yorker and Time weekly magazines and PBS TV. His assistant called to make appointments for max 2 a day, and not more than one hour each. Also he told her to apologize for the other callers due scheduling issues.

The New York Times was scheduled the same day in the afternoon, followed by New York Post at 11:am the next day, and the New Yorker magazine at 3:00 pm. The time magazine was scheduled at 11:00 am the following day and the PBS interview in the afternoon. The setting was in his conference room adjacent to his office.

The questions asked were pretty much the same in every interview, asking how and why the incident happened, what to do with the sentencing money, and what he hoped to achieve from the future organization. Freddie saved the best for the important interview with PBS on Thursday. The interviewer was seasoned in matters of personal relationships and was calm in handling the recording. There were two cameramen from different angles to film the interview with Freddie dressed in a suit, sitting across from the interviewer that introduced him,

> "I am here with Fredric Rodman, who some of you are already familiar with his name and his story. Freddie, as he likes to be called, owns and runs a real estate company in New York and agreed to share with us the highlights of his episode. He agreed to answer few questions, so let us begin. Freddie, can you briefly tell us what happened?"

"Sure. As you may have heard already, I was kidnapped and beaten harshly about 10 days ago. I am almost healed from injuries to my rib cage in my chest. This incident occurred due to my refusal to pay them $2 million ransom because I abruptly broke up my relationship with a lady I was dating at that time. The kidnappers were eventually caught, and they admitted that the lady that sued me was the one who was behind the unlawful demand for money, as well as the kidnapping that followed. That surprised me, as I didn't think that she could do that on her own.

"During the court hearing, she confessed that she was not alone in the whole scheme. When asked by my lawyer whom else was involved in the plan, she pointed at, and stated the name of, her own legal representative, who was sitting next to her at the defendant's desk in the courtroom. That shocked everyone present, including the judge. Her lawyer was asked by the judge to take the chair for questioning, but he took the 5th and refused to say anything. He was held in contempt and stayed behind bars that night.

"The next day, the accused lawyer confessed that he was the one who pushed the lady to execute the ugly plan. However he denied that there were other partners in his firm that were involved. My astute lawyer and his team did thorough investigation that showed, with proof, that the two other partners in the law firm were involved in similar cases like mine for three years in a row. The judge arranged for the FBI to raid their offices, arrest them and confiscate their files. With the evidence the judge had received, he then imposed the sentences that were publically announced that day."

"Thank you Freddie for this clear description of the events. I am sure many of our viewers would like to know what you intend to do with the $1.2 million you were awarded by the 2 judges in Queens and in Manhattan?" The interviewer asked.

"I already started the registration of a non-profit organization I call DAA, which stands for "Dignity Above All'. The *money will be deposited in its account, plus, I also decided to add another $1 million from my own money to ensure the feasibility and success of the project I have in mind."* Freddie replied.

"Can you kindly elaborate on what you have in mind?" Freddie was asked.

"I thought about 7 goals to try and achieve, these are:

1. *To bring awareness to young women to avoid, on their own, or if approached by others, seductive and harassment acts with well-to-do men who could be vulnerable to fall in their traps, as I did.*
2. *To provide these women who agree to join DAA, the proper guidance and education to seek other alternatives, with greater dignity and self-esteem.*
3. *To help find respectable jobs for these women with their skills or with new skills from the education programs they will receive from DAA.*
4. *To ask the ones we help out, to pledge continued assistance to DAA by attracting other women they know, not to be tempted to go the other way, and recruit others to spread the word.*
5. *To create a weekly publication that will reach all national subscribers to DAA, with professional opinions and articles, alerting readers how to avoid potential damages that could occur as a result of their negligence.*
6. *To bring awareness to men also, about the values of loyalty, by not pursuing relationships outside their marriage as they could end up destroying their family units by going through ugly divorces. I would be the best witness to confirm this truth. And,*
7. *To try and create other DAA centers in major cities around the nation, and to raise funds to cover additional expansion costs."*

"Wow Freddie! what a noble task you have waiting for you. A last personal question, if I may. Has your wife expressed any remarks about what you went through, and do you intend to reconcile and get back together?" The interviewer asked.

"Interesting question! The answer is not yet. I would love for us to reconcile and for the mother of my two boys, to forgive my stupid behavior, now that I am in a much better place in my life. I would like to share with every one that the suffering we go through in life, can be looked upon as an opportunity to know who we are, and to cross over to the other side of enlightenment and peace." Freddie stated compassionately.

"Thank you so much for this enlightening interview Freddie and we wish you great success with your new endeavors."

Freddie felt good after the interview and hoped its message will resonate with many people. He was told he would be advised within short about the date and time the station will broadcast the interview.

***

"Welcome... to the Man of the Week!" I told Freddie when he walked in to my place for dinner Thursday evening, as planned.

We hugged and Freddie greeted and kissed Melody on the cheek when she walked out of the kitchen. Freddie said,

"Thanks for having me, it's been a busy week."

I had saved copies of the two newspaper articles and handed them over to Freddie saying,

"It seems that way! These were great articles about your interview with the papers... New York city has a new celebrity now! We are all proud of you and um... your courage to share the truth. Do you others coming up?" I asked.

"I'm done with five already including two magazines and one interview with PBS." Freddie said,

"PBS? Wow! That's a very respectable TV network. When did you do that Freddie?"

"This afternoon… they said they'd let me know when they'll broadcast it. I have to admit, I also used the occasion to--to promote my new organization DAA." Freddie said.

"Yeah, that's wonderful Freddie, Barry told me… and I hope we can all help you to launch it." Melody said loudly, form the kitchen.

"Thanks Melody!"

"I was also asked if I am considering to--to reconcile, or go back with Matilda."

"And?" I asked curiously.

"And what? I said I'm trying… and it's not up to me only." Freddie answered confidently.

"That's a good start, the whole world knows now you're trying and she'll get the message as well. By the way, she called me yesterday to see how you're doing. She read the same articles too… She didn't say much but I sensed that um… she's softening her stance towards you and that you're being forgiven? I said with a smile.

"Don't joke with me Barry… she sensed it or she told you so?"

"I'm happy you're so eager to know Freddie, that's a good sign. I see reconciliation coming our way soon. Wouldn't you welcome it?" I quizzed.

"Barry stop guessing. I said it publically that I'm trying… she has to be willing to!"

"Do you see yourself back together?" I directly asked.

"Hey guys can you two hold this discussion for 5 more minutes and, we all talk at the table?" Melody shouted from the kitchen.

"OK fine! We'll wait for you… let's eat already, I'm hungry."

"Five minutes Barry… Five! Control yourself." Melody said.

We both laughed and held back our talk until Melody walked out with meatloaf that smelled so good. Once she put it in the middle of the table she invited us to come and take our seats. I opened a bottle of red wine and we toasted Freddie for looking good and healthy again. I cut the meat and served it with some mashed potatoes and salad on the side. Then Melody spoke,

"OK now we can talk… what were you saying about you and Matilda, whom I have yet to meet?"

"Ask your curious 'lover boy' here… he'll tell you everything… he knows more than anybody else what will happen that's why I love him." Freddie said jokingly.

"So, lover boy! Tell me." Melody demanded.

"I just asked Freddie a simple question! I asked him if he sees himself back with Matilda? And… I would like an answer." I said.

There were few moments of silence and everyone was looking at every one else. Then Freddie broke the silence and said,

"I've become more mature as of late… If I were to be in a new relationship I assure you, as I assure myself, that I would be loyal and committed to—to the one I'm with. As it pertains to Matilda, the anger and the hurt she suffered from, may still be deep? I have forgiven myself already! I am not sure that she has forgiven me?

"And, supposing that she has, I'm not sure I—I would be too excited to be back with her… for reasons other than to be closer to the boys. The boys will eventually become of age and leave… then I ask myself, even now in your presence, do I still love her to the degree that I want to spend the rest of my life with her? Will it be any different, as a second round? I don't know the answer to that yet… I need more time to consider." Freddie said truthfully. There was silence again until Melody spoke and she said,

"Freddie, I don't know you well enough like Barry does, but I tell you, hum… you're more in touch with yourself nowadays, and you are fully entitled to think it over."

I then added,

"Would you like me to feel her out… while you are considering the whole thing?"

"I don't believe so, Barry. If it's meant for us to talk it out, it has to be initiated by her… not by me, or even interceded by you. She knows where I stand. I asked her before, and she refused to play along… I would let it simmer for a while and see what the future holds in store. I'm not in a rush anymore! With her, or any one else?" Freddie expressed his true feelings about this.

"Just to be clear, and I'm your best friend, is the ghost of Anne still intercepting your thoughts?" I courageously asked.

"Barry, ghosts live in the subconscious mind… she could still be there, prodding and exploring… but I have told my self consciously that I should try and forget her… I made that decision when she told me that she's um… not ready for a relationship with any man, including me. So what do you want to say? I need to protect myself from a potential heartbreak. But, she's always in mind I must admit.

"Lately though, she's been hinting that she misses me and stuff… She says she admires the fact that I learn fast and she's highly impressed by the positive transformation of my mind and my continued inner search for my true self. Last time we spoke, she even told me that as her previous student I have already bypassed her … and she's willing to learn from me now." Freddie explained.

"But, if circumstances allow, can you hum… see yourself living with her the rest of your life?" I asked.

"Yes I can!" Freddie responded quickly.

"I see! Then let's leave it to the Universe to guide you." I said.

"OK now, enough about me, tell me about you guys, when are you getting married? Freddie asked joyfully.

"It'll be soon within the next three months… but we have not fixed the date yet." I clarified.

"Melody, are you sure… you want to marry this lover boy?

"You bet I want to, Freddie, I love him deeply. You're going to be the best man, who else? That's exciting!" Melody declared lovingly.

"Thanks again for a lovely evening and a sumptuous meal Melody… you have truly outdid yourself!" Freddie stood up and ready to leave. He gave them both big hugs and said goodnight.

***

It was close to 10 pm when Freddie left and he checked his mobile phone, which he had on silent. There was a message from Anne which he quickly answered saying he was having dinner with Barry and Melody and if he could call her back in 15 minutes when he's at the hotel. Anne immediately answered "no problem".

Once settled in his suite he sat down on a chair in the living area. It has been few days since they spoke. He called Anne who picked up and said,

"Hello Fredric… my new hero! People don't stop talking about you, my NY friend is a famous guy now."

"How are you Anne? You must have read the news online, right?"

"I read your NYT interview on Tuesday, what a delivery? You did a great job! I'm so overwhelmed… with the news about your DAA, and its purpose. What a character transformation? You were truly impressive I admire you so much more now. Who else interviewed you?" Anne said and asked.

"A total of five, including some magazines, and I finished with PBS this afternoon."

"PBS, my favorite TV station… when will they broadcast it, I want to see it and… and your adorable face." Anne proudly said.

"They'll tell me soon. I'll let you know."

"Freddie, I can't get over your plan, um… You becoming an activist, helping out women and men. I've never been proud of anyone as much as I'm proud of you now… How do you plan to manage this organization?" Anne asked curiously.

"I don't know yet… This afternoon, with PBS I outlined 7 goals I would like to-- to achieve, as a result of creating this task. I am also adding another $1 million from my pocket… to express how serious I am about its purpose. I wish you're here… to help me launch it." Freddie asked.

"Do you think I can help you? How?" Anne asked.

"Don't underestimate yourself… I say it again and again! If you're interested, and I'm not kidding, I--I would appoint you to be the CEO of this organization… and I'm certain you'll do an excellent job running it. You are a self-starter and an entrepreneur. Name your price and you have it…Listen, you helped me to find out who I am, to go within and learn how to love myself, and now it's our turn to help others… and experience true love by extending mine to other people.

"This incidence that I went through opened my eyes and taught me a lot. Knowing you… and reading the books you sent me, helped me tremendously to--to discover the truth about myself. I am a good man, and I appreciate God's gifts… It's time I pay back my dues. So please consider being by my side. It would be the greatest honor bestowed upon me." Freddie said passionately.

There was long silence on the other end. Freddie wondered where Anne went. Then she suddenly said,

"I'm sorry I had to wipe out my tears first… you made me cry! These are tears of joy… because you flatter me and honor me much more than I deserve. I'm crying because I did not treat you in kind, when you told me how much you liked me… I've been a fool and an arrogant bit…, (forgive me for saying it), and I profusely apologize. You say I've been good to you… how? By advising you with words and sending you books? You deserve much more… and I'm sorry I didn't open my heart to you… Please forgive me!" Anne said while still sobbing.

"Anne, please stop! You are an amazing person and don't ever apologize to me. I don't blame you for not opening your heart at that time… I was in shambles too, and suffering from despair and low self-esteem. You, yes-- you… helped me to change, and I'm eternally grateful to that. I owe you my transformation for being the person I am today and I can't thank you enough. The universe sent you to me at the right time." Freddie said emphatically.

"Fredric, my darling, allow me to say 'I love you'. I truly mean it. You brought joy to my life… The love, care and gentlemanly respect you showed me, when we were together, was unprecedented. You are the kind of man I—I dream to be with. Are you serious um… about wanting me next to you to help you?" Anne asked.

"I've never been more serious… Are you kidding? Not only we will have great success, but we will have fun together as well. I'm thinking aloud now… Hear me for a minute… How about um… we move together into a beautiful apartment in Manhattan? You can choose the one you like from many that I own… And you decorate it the way you like. Then I find a big office space, around 5000 sq. ft. of which we carve out a big space for you… consisting of two sections, one to treat patients clinically, as your own business, and the other as CEO of DAA organization. You can staff it with as many managers and employees as you want. Besides, I'm now officially divorced, and we can discuss if marriage is what we both can agree upon. No pressure. What do you say?" Freddie said spontaneously.

"Mamma Madonna! Are you sure you're not under the influence of something you took? You mean you'll do all that for me? Are you crazy? Do you love me too?" Anne asked soberly.

"First I'm not under the influence of any alcohol or drugs… I am a new man now, remember? Secondly, yes you deserve all that and much more. Thirdly, yes I love you… You should have noticed how much I loved you um… when I first laid my eyes on you. So here we are, what do we do next?" Freddie said affectionately.

"Fredric, my sweetheart (wow! It sounds right to say it now), this has been an amazing conversation… I thought you were half-joking when you asked me about it the last time we spoke. Allow me to digest it and sleep on it. I'll call you tomorrow… I give you a big kiss and a big hug. Have sweet dreams!" Anne expressed softly before she hung up.

"You too, my dear!"

***

I had a call from Freddie the next morning at 8:00 am. I had just come out of the shower and still undressed to go to work.

"What is it Freddie, are you suffering from insomnia… or food poisoning?" I asked.

"Listen … I know it's early and you're getting ready to go to work. I briefly wanted to tell you that Anne called me last night after I left your place… She heard about the interviews, and read the one in NYT. She was mostly impressed with the DAA project… I challenged her to consider coming to New York and become the CEO of DAA. To make a long story short, she…she told me she loved me and I echoed her expression to the word. She said she'd sleep on it and let me know later in the day. So, there you have it."

"Freddie… you never stop to amaze me with your life stories, you certainly are not a boring friend at all… are you sure this is what you want? What if--if she agrees to come to New York, to start a new practice and head your organization? Are you ready to have her in your life again, and will you live together?" I asked while I was still drying myself.

"Yes!" Freddie answered.

"That's a quick answer… Wow! Then go for it. Love has its own mysteries. Good luck and we will talk this evening. Bye."

***

Freddie had his children for the weekend. He missed seeing them for two weeks. He was happy to see how delighted they were to see him too. He noticed how his relationship with them had turned around substantially and that observation reduced the feelings of guild with him equally. During lunch together on Saturday, Brian his older boy asked his father,

"Dad, Mom said that you were in the papers earlier this week, what was that all about?"

"Well, it's a long story but in short, I decided to start a new non-profit organization that um… would help women to refrain from seducing men who are emotionally weak. What happens is that it causes a break up with their wives… and creates a dysfunctional atmosphere for the children to grow up in. This is what happened to me! The woman I had befriended after I left home, (which was terribly wrong as I look back) sued me after I broke up with her, and I won the case. The judge awarded me with enough money to--to start the organization. So my story… attracted the attention of the media." Freddie explained.

"Mom also said that what you will be doing is a heroic act and no other man has done such a thing before." Brian added.

"Maybe… I don't know. What matters is that I truly want to try and fix the wrong that some men do, and hope it will keep them back at home with their families." Freddie said.

"That's great Dad… we're proud of you." Brian expressed.

"Any chance you will be coming back home, Dad?" The younger boy, Mark innocently asked.

"I'm trying first to--to develop a friendly relationship with your Mom… and then it's a question for both of us to discuss and see if it is workable."

"Yeah… but do you want to?" young Mark asked again.

"Look, your mother is a very good women and I respect her a lot, she has to also agree. As for me… I'll do anything to be physically closer to you guys." Freddie replied.

"Dad, I think Mom is seeing another man." Brian said.

"Well, it's her right! As you may know we are officially divorced… and she's free to see other men. It's fully her choice. Regardless whom she sees however, I—I know your mother, she loves you more than anybody else in the world… and she won't let anyone-- I mean anyone-- take this priority away from her. Trust me and you'll see!" Freddie explained.

"Mark and I love you both very much, Dad." Brain confirmed.

"That's what I love to hear… we both love you more guys!" Freddie reconfirmed.

They had a lot of fun, through Sunday afternoon. They went to the zoo in the park, went to the movies and saw Star Wars, went shopping for books of their choice at the big book store on fifth avenue, had dinner at their favorite restaurant, and played card games and Monopoly in the hotel suite.

Anne had not called or left a message since Thursday night, but Freddie was not concerned knowing she had a lot to think about. He thought he might give her a call on Sunday evening.

CHAPTER 10

A Definite Awakening

Soon after the kids left on Sunday afternoon Freddie called Anne.

"Good evening my dear, is everything alright?"

"I'm fine sweetheart! I've been totally immersed um… with my thoughts, eva … evaluating the last conversation we had. You know, it's not easy for me to--to leave Madison after all these years. I did a lot of hard work the last 14 years, studying and working… So, I've been digging deep within, to see if there were other feelings hiding in the dark rooms of my mind… and look the amount of light required to--to bring them out to the surface." Anne explained passionately.

"I understand it's not easy… this is a normal reaction whenever a move from one city to the other is considered. Tell me about the hidden feelings you're talking about if you may!" Freddie asked.

"First, let me say that I would be comfortable with the work or the responsibility of the task at hand. The thing is more about you and me living together, plus a possible marriage and stuff… That's were I am struggling within. Besides, we only spent one week together… we don't know each other well enough… wouldn't it be a bit scary if all of a sudden we move in together?" Anne said elaborately.

"Anne, my dear let's look at this one thing at a time… you mentioned three different situations in what you just said. The first one about work seems not to be an issue, and that's good. The thing about living together can also be resolved… We don't have to live together, until you—you know what you want for sure. You can live alone in any of the many apartments I own in the city, free rent. Thirdly, and as it pertains to the idea of marriage we can put this on the shelf for now. We leave this to the Universe to decide… How about that?" Freddie explained to ease her concerns.

"You're such a good salesman! You focus on the solution, not the problem. I admit I still have fears um… when it comes to a new relationship with a man. The last one I had was highly disappointing and I—I promised myself not to do it again. Please understand… It is that fear also that pushed me to try it out with another woman, knowing it is not what I preferred." Anne expressed truthfully.

"Hear me! You are a smart women, and I'm sure you know a lot about the power of visualization… when it comes to considering a new situation. In fact, I learned about that from one of the books you sent me. How about you visualizing the scene when you and I spent the week together? If you enjoyed it, why not visualize us doing a repeat performance for a much longer period of time? Would that help you to find out if you can do it? Please take your time to decide." Freddie suggested compassionately.

"You… You… you're good you! I love it. You are a fast learner indeed. As I told you last time, I'll be glad to be your student… It's definitely a good exercise for the mind, and I—I also believe in the power of visualization. Let me try it out for a week or so! Meanwhile, how was your weekend with the kids?" Anne said happily.

"It was good, they left about an hour ago. We had a great time and… their mother told them I was in the papers. They were curious to know why. So I told them in simple words why, and then they said they love me. What more can I ask for? I'm grateful!" Freddie responded.

"Good! Any further gossip on your story?" Anne asked.

"well… on Friday more people asked to meet me, but I refused. I need a break I think… PBS called me though, saying the interview will be on the air this Tuesday at 7 pm, that's if you care to watch it."

"You bet I will professor! I give you a big hug now and… will talk soon." Anne said.

"Have a great evening… and you're always in my mind! Good night." Freddie responded before they hung up.

***

Freddie called me after he hung up with Anne. He told me about the conversation he just had with her. He repeated that she seemed reluctant to consider the move to New York. I asked why and he said,

"She seems to be concerned about entering into a--a new relationship with another man. She said she had a terrible time with her ex-husband and she promised herself not to marry again." Freddie said.

"How do you feel about that? Then what if it's a no go?" I asked.

"I don't know yet… It's not the end of the world! But, other than the fact that I—I really would love for us to live together, and may be get married one day… the thing is, she's perfect for the job. She's very smart, entrepreneurial, highly educated and… a psychologist on top of that, and all women can relate to her." Freddie stated.

"Did you offer her the job as CEO of DAA?' I asked.

"Yes, Barry! I did and she said work is not an issue she can be very comfortable handling the job… I also offered her a space for her own private practice, and a free apartment if she's not ready to move in with me, and a compensation package of her own choice, what more could I do?" Freddie explained.

"You've done more than enough… if you ask me. As the saying goes, 'you can take the horse to the water but you can't force him to drink'. Just give her time… If she meant it when she told you she loved you, then leave it at that. Love, my friend, is--is the most powerful force in the world. If Love does not change her mind, nothing else would… That's for sure!" I emphasized.

"You're right Barry! I am now leaving it to destiny… I had enough conflicts of my own already, I don't need another one. The ball is in her court, to decide how and where she wants to live her life." Freddie responded.

"That's good! Anything else?" I asked.

"I had a great time with the boys this weekend… and they told me Matilda briefed them on the--the write-up in the papers about me. Mark, the younger one, asked me if I would go back home now… I said it's not fully up to me. Brian then mentioned that his mom could be seeing another man. I told him she's entitled to do what she wants she's a free woman… So, that's the latest." Freddie said.

"Well… yeah! I didn't want to tell you earlier. When we invited you to dinner at our place on Thursday we wanted to see if we could surprise you. I asked Matilda if she could join us for dinner. She asked me if you were invited too… I told her the truth. And then she immediately said, it wouldn't be appropriate because she has a new man in her life… So, now you know!" I said.

"It's OK, Barry! As I told the kids, she's free to do what she wants… Perhaps now it would be easier for us to be friends, and—and would make it easier for me to—to see the kids more frequently, on weekends, or during the week… This gives her a chance to also see her boyfriend more frequently. Right?" Freddie calculated.

"Yes, you may be right … it's possible. Why don't I call her and feel her out discretely?" I suggested.

"Go ahead, find out! It wouldn't hurt. By the way, PBS will be on this coming Tuesday at 7 pm. Watch it and tell me what you think. Say hi to Melody. Bye for now!"

***

The New Yorker and Time magazines came out on Monday. The articles were written favorably and 'Fredric Rodman' was given new titles as a *'Corruption Terminator'* in one and a *' DAA for Young Women'* in another. Both articles had a brief Bio of Freddie and his photo attached. His receptionist received many calls asking to speak to him and his assistant took note of who called without disturbing him. Some of them said they would like to become volunteers in DAA. Others called from distant cities, asking for phone interviews with Freddie. The rest said they'd call back.

Freddie became popular in many circles of New York. He remained calm and humble, and did not let this new recognition get to his head. He remained focused on the task at hand and pushed James, his lawyer, to expedite the registration of DAA. He also checked with his managers to find him the right location in Manhattan for DAA headquarters.

Additionally, he asked his people to check any vacant big apartments in Midtown Manhattan. He told them to check their files and notify him immediately, before they're rented. He was literally committed to a new and better change in his life. His excitement about the new organization, and the continued success of his business lifted him up. He wished he could have Anne by his side to share his new life. She was instrumental in helping him achieve this transformation with her loving wisdom and outright advice. He gave Anne time to contemplate her move and her inner thoughts.

In the middle of the day, Freddie had a call from James who told him that his colleague visited Jane in Jail, an hour away from Manhattan. He said that she was cooperative and liked the idea of a possible reduction of her term in prison. She said she would gladly help out as an active member of DAA when she gets released. Then James added,

"Now I can't guarantee she will live up to her word if she gets out sooner, Freddie. However, it's worth asking the judge if he could reopen the case since we were the ones who charged her to begin with. My colleague also said she looked frail and thin… evidently she's stressed out, and would welcome an earlier release. She even said she'd work for free at DAA in return to our gesture not to ask for money. This process would take a—a couple of month to implement… So I believe we should get started, if you're still um… in the mood to help her out."

"Yes James, go ahead!" Freddie responded.

"Fine, and I'll keep you advised on DAA registration."

***

Two of his managers walked in around 4 pm the same day and told Freddie that a good-sized apartment on the East side would be vacant in two weeks. It is in a very good condition, and beautifully decorated with very good quality furniture. The size was 2750 livable sq. ft. with three bedrooms en suite a library and a large living dining area with an open kitchen. The apartment has panoramic view of the East River, queens and part of Brooklyn from the 23rd floor. The location is on 53rd street between first and second avenues.

"Whose building is it?" Freddie asked.

"Yours!"

"Oops! Thanks for reminding me… yeah, now I remember. Check it out and save it for me. When it is vacated let me know, I want to see it myself. How about the office space?" Freddie asked.

"That's a bit more complicated… we can't find an empty space in any of the modern buildings you own. But there is an old and beautiful large town house of 4900 sq. ft. on 56th street between Madison and Park avenues available in about one month. It has 4 floors and a basement, but with an elevator. Actually the lower two floors are quite spacious and suitable for very elegant offices. The basement is big and perfect for storage, a small cafeteria/kitchen and for filing cabinets.

"The space needs some modification to create more offices or open space for employees. It has a good entrance, reception area and four big rooms for executive offices and a conference room on the lower levels. you can see it tomorrow, our tenants wouldn't mind."

"Yes, I want to see it please. Ask the architect to join us."

***

While the managers were still in Freddie's office, his assistant rushed in and whispered something in his ears. He told her, "in the conference room". Then he asked the managers to Please leave.

He walked in the conference room adjacent to his office, and there she was, sitting at one end of the table, smiling. It was his ex wife, Matilda! He said,

"What a surprise? What brings you here, is everything alright?"

"I came to see you… it's been a long time. You look good and healthy thank God! I wanted to surprise you. Barry called me and said we should be friends, and I agree. So I come here in peace to extend my friendship to you… for our peace of mind and for the sake of our children." Matilda explained gently.

"Now that's a good surprise to hear you say, that is music to my ears… I welcome your gesture and thank you for it." Freddie responded happily.

"The children tell me they are having a good time with you on your weekends and as a good gesture on my part I--I would like you to feel free to see them anytime you want, including week nights as well. They need you as a father… and you are their idol."

"Matilda, I can't thank you enough… I really appreciate it. I hope that you are less angry with me nowadays, and… forgive me for the terrible hurt I foolishly caused you. Thank God for the wisdom he bestowed upon you to—to allow me to share the love and the responsibility we both have for our two boys. I--I truly would like us to be good friends." Freddie said gratefully.

"In the spirit of this occasion, I also want you to hear it directly from me, I am seeing another man!" Matilda said eagerly.

"That's also good news! We both have to—to move on. All I wish is that um he respects you and gives you the honest love you deserve. And, that he treats the boys well, respecting the fact that I am their father, not him." Freddie responded.

"I can assure you that no one um… will take your place as their father. I'm also happy to hear the good news I—I read in the papers and I want to say how proud I am of what you're doing. What a difference a day makes?" Matilda said.

"Well it has been a unique experience for me lately. The incident, the pain and the recovery, all led me to search within and find out who I am. I transformed into becoming a better person. I gave a good interview on PBS you may want to watch it, even with the children, on Tuesday at 7 pm… It would reveal nothing but the truth! I fear nothing anymore, and I—I'm in a good place in my life now." Freddie said mindfully.

Matilda smiled, stood up and said,

"I'm so grateful I came to mend fences with you. I wish you the best of life… and please feel free to call me anytime you wish. I look forward to our new friendship, and thank you for blessing my new relationship. His name is John by the way… he is a medical doctor. Perhaps you'll have a chance to meet him soon."

"I look forward to that! And thanks again… for this pleasant surprise. Love to the kids… Come give me a hug!" Freddie said, and they gave each other a friendly hug and said goodbye.

As soon as Matilda left, Freddie called me and said,

"You rascal you! You did it and I'm grateful. She just left and will talk later."

"Le's talk now, I have a couple of minutes, how was it?" I asked.

"It went very well, and a real surprise! We spoke calmly… she told me about John, her new boy friend the doctor… She congratulated me on my current events. She also said I can see the kids anytime I want, and for me to feel free to call her anytime. So all is well… and thanks, buddy!"

"I'm very happy to hear that and I'm sure you'll sleep better tonight." I said.

"You bet! Thanks again and good night!"

***

Freddie went to see the potential office space for DAA with one of his managers and the architect after work. The space was still occupied, but the tenants allowed them to se it. They spent 30 minutes touring the floors and taking notes of what changes would be required to accommodate a large staff and offices for three senior executives. Freddie liked it and thought it gives a homey atmosphere to the visitors and employees of this ne w humanitarian organization. He agreed with the architect on the few modifications that would two take two weeks to finish before it becomes operational.

He also asked to see the apartment recommended to move into, at noon the next day. He was happy he'd be moving out of the hotel soon. Within few minutes of his arrival to the hotel Anne called Freddie. She said,

"Hi Fredric, these new thoughts are dizzying… It would be best if we could see each other soon, and talk face-to-face."

"I couldn't agree more, sweet angel! How about this weekend? Can you come Friday and leave Monday evening? I –I would fly over myself… but there are few things I would like you to see!" Freddie suggested.

"Uh ha! I would have to check my schedule… and clear it for two days then. I'll get back to you… Let's not discuss anything now. I still have some more soul-searching to do." Anne stipulated.

"Great! I'll send you the tickets… text me the itinerary when you get it."

"No problem my dear! I can manage it on my own. I'll get back to you soon." Anne responded.

"Fine! Don't book a hotel, you'll stay here with me, okay?" Freddie demanded.

"OK! Will text you … Hugs and kisses. Bye for now."

"Bye, don't forget to watch PBS tomorrow!" Freddie said before he hung up.

***

Freddie had the evening for himself. He decided to stay in and reflect on the progress of events that were taking place. He pulled out his journal to write down his thoughts,

Only few weeks ago since I started shifting from moments of despair and suffering to a new road of good awakening. A new beginning is awaiting me, though unexpected, but exciting. The dark rooms of my mind see the light now. The physical pain inflicted upon me healed my inner wounds and enlightened me with hope and love.

I am experiencing several changes in my midlife. I am not only physically healthier but also spiritually and emotionally more aware. The inspiration to create a new humanitarian organization to help others is fulfilling. I am at peace with myself, and the guilt within me has subsided. My civil rapport with Matilda is being regained. My decision to forgive and ease Jane's pain is merciful. My relationship with my children is on the rise. My relationship with Barry and my staff remains solid. And my hopeful relationship with Anne is surrendered to Destiny.

I will be moving out of the hotel soon to start living a normal new life. I will wear another hat to run the new organization DAA, while I pray that Anne will be guided to come and take it over. I would love to have Anne by my side, also as a partner in my life. I will not be anxious as I am content with whatever decision she makes. I am grateful to the great blessings bestowed upon me regardless."

While he was inspired, Freddie also wrote a poem,

> *I always wondered if soon I find*
> *The partner imagined in my mind*
> *After a year of twists and error*
> *But now my search ends for better*
> *I hope I found the hidden catch*
> *Who saw in me the right match*
> *I'll treat her well with no demand*
> *As she Always helps me understand*

We walk the twilight and sip our wine
We thank the heavens for our dime
The sunset fades but not her smile
My love for her lasts a long while

I dare not make another wrong
And learn the tune of her song
It comes once, so be aware
A moment to cherish and not to spare

No more errors and no more search
I moved forward holding the torch
I closed the door to all my fears
And said goodbye to all my tears

He went ahead and emailed it to Anne, hoping its spirit would introduce more comfort during her soul-searching. Few minutes later Anne called and said,

"Oh my goodness! ... You are amazing, where did you hide this poetic gift. I love it and I—I love you."

"I'm glad you like it. I always wanted to write poems, but I needed someone in my life to—to inspire me... Besides, if I didn't learn how to--to love myself first, I couldn't express my love to others... I hope you take it with a grain of salt, and I don't intend to interfere with your inner mission at this stage... I—I was writing in my journal, and the thought hit me. It's from the heart." Freddie commented.

"You are truly one of a kind! I can't get over it. I read it twice and tears cascaded down my cheeks. I am really touched by your prose and honest feelings. I'm sure I—I will sleep smiling and dreaming about us. I kiss you and I hug you... I'll let you know tomorrow about my flight schedule. Thanks again my sweet Romeo!" Anne said with joy.

"Good night my dearest Juliet, will talk soon."

Freddie was happy. He ordered some food to eat, and spent an hour online to learn how to run a non-profit organization. He then went to sleep with positive thoughts racing in his mind.

CHAPTER 11

A Brighter Side Of The Moon

PBS broadcast for Freddie's interview was at 7 pm on Tuesday. Millions of people in America tuned in to this popular news station. It was expected to make a lot of noise in the nation, but not to the high level it reached. All law firms and lawyers in the U.S. and Canada must have watched it too. Even Freddie's mother with whom he rarely connects said she watched the show with a group of her lady friends, during a bridge tournament in her country club.

Freddie was alone in his hotel living room when the show started. He was pleased that it was presented without any editing or modifications. The whole thing lasted 15 minutes, including three minutes about Freddie the person and his background. The reporter emphasized how 'daring' Fredric Rodman took such an unprecedented action to help women become more aware. Also, putting up big amounts of money to teach them and train them with new skills.

Two minutes after the broadcast was finished, Freddie's phone rang and it was Anne who said,

"Congratulations! You did a great job and the whole nation is proud of you. I am honored that I know you... Sir! I invited my friend who came with her new boy friend to listen to the interview... and I also bragged about how handsome and smart you are. They were very impressed. I just wanted to call you to congratulate you now. I will text you my itinerary after they leave. Bye!"

Freddie hardly had time to say goodbye to her. Anne had to go back to her friends.

Then I called,

"Did you pop the champagne yet?" I started.

"No, I'm waiting for you to join me."

"Freddie, it was great… what you said and how you handled yourself is exemplary, my heroic friend, I am so proud of you… and I bet you the whole world will respond positively to—to this interview. You're a Star! Hollywood will chase you for a movie soon, you'll see!"

"Well we'll see! I need to remain focused on getting the work started… I'm excited about the new project, I must admit! I'm now reserving an apartment for me on the East side, and an office space in a townhouse I liked nearby. We need to begin soon, while the momentum is alive and hot. I—I must deliver on my promises." Freddie stated.

"Did Anne call you? Has she decided yet? You asked her to join you, no?" I asked.

"Yeah, she called! She had her friends watching the interview too and said she'd call me later… She asked for us to meet in person as her mind is still clouded um… with conflicting thoughts. She's coming this weekend for more discussions, face-to-face." Freddie said.

"I'm sure you understand what she's going through. It's not easy to make quick decisions to--to pack her stuff and leave at your beck-on call. She has roots and many clients in Madison. And, she's the type that wouldn't turn her back suddenly on people. I advise you um…not to push her to come quickly. Give her time, may be six more month if need be, If her heart is with you, she'll come eventually… Let her figure out what to do with her practice, to sell it to another psychoanalyst or transfer her clients to other practitioners. This is a slow procedure… It could take few months to achieve. If the two of you are committed as a couple in the interim, you can both visit one another every other weekend, or so. Consider her as your partner serving in the army overseas. I don't need to go on telling you what to do now… I'm sure you got the picture." I said lengthily.

"I hear you Barry, if I push her she'll disappear. I'll make sure she doesn't receive any pressure from me. Thanks for the advice anyhow! Let's get together soon… Say hi to Melody for me."

Freddie cut me off he said he had another incoming call, from Matilda. They spoke for 4 minutes. She told him the boys are so proud of their 'honest and loving father'. He thanked her for her call and then took few moments to rest his mind.

An hour later Freddie received a text message from Anne with her flight schedule on Thursday, 7 pm at La Guardia. He texted her back saying he'll pick her up at the airport. He was happy she'll be staying for 4 nights and was looking forward to seeing her again. He will make plans to show her both the apartment and the office space on Friday.

***

The next two days in the office were buzzing with the phones ringing all the time. Two assistants were assigned to take messages. They were mostly addressed to Freddie, asking for interviews. Some were from old business associates he dealt with.

James called directly on his mobile phone and told him he watched the interview on PBS and was impressed. He then added,

"The organization is almost registered officially… We also opened a bank account for DAA. How about the office space and its location? They will ask me for a physical address."

"I realize that, you'll get it in 48 hours. We need to consider staffing it also. I may use some of my current employees to help temporarily. I will be registered as the founder and chairman of the board I assume. I'd like you to be the counsel and a member of the board please. I'm not sure about the CEO position and other managers yet… I will keep you advised. By the way, Matilda and I are communicating well together. Please don't forget to ask the Judge about Jane." Freddie enumerated his agenda to James.

"Noted… and will revert soon about Judge Lumen. I left him a message already. I will check when the first Million from Mr. Padowski will be released from his frozen account. Anything else? James asked

"Not for now, thank you James."

Freddie's assistant came to his office with 16 messages from different callers. He went through them and shoved aside the unknown l ones. The remaining 9 messages were from media companies, including one from the London Times. He told her he would agree to a max 10 minutes each phone interviews, and to schedule them all before Thursday 5 pm. He asked her not to take any more messages the rest of the week.

Apart from attending to his real estate business, he spent 2 hours each day, Wednesday and Thursday with phone interviews, to make sure the rest of the week he gives his full attention to Anne's visit.

The flight arrived at La Guardia airport from Madison on time. Freddie waited for Anne at the gate for 15 minutes then saw her gracefully walking out with a rolling suitcase. He walked towards her and met her half way. They hugged and kissed. The chauffeur of the limousine was waiting for to take them to the hotel. They sat in the back seat holding hands and looking at one another with big smiles and short conversations.

They both expressed how happy they were to see each other again. They knew they have a lot to talk about. It was close to 8 pm by the time they arrived at the hotel and Freddie suggested dinner in the suite. She agreed and asked to draw a bath and relax in her bathrobe. He ordered the food they chose, plus a bottle of champagne and Caspian caviar to start, and a good bottle of wine with the food.

The waiter came and placed the food at the dining table with the proper plates and glasses, with a small bouquet of flowers in the middle of the table. Freddie dimmed the lights in the room and lit few scented candles to provide a romantic atmosphere for the evening. Then Anne came out from the bathroom looking gorgeous. She had make up on her face, and wore high heels and a sexy set of lingerie, under her open bathrobe. Freddie tried his best to control his excitement. She looked like a living goddess.

They sat down at the table and he handed her a chilled glass of champagne. They clicked their glasses and he welcomed her officially with a soft kiss on her lips. He served her caviar on blinis while sipping the champagne and having small talk. As the edge of being together was gone with the help of champagne, she brought up the subject of his interview, and thanked him again for the beautiful poem he wrote. Freddie listened attentively, smiling back at her, and expressing how happy he was to have her with him. Then he spoke and said,

"You know sweetheart, when we first met, we spent our time getting to know each other. This time, and after several discussions we had on the phone, it feels like… we've known each other for years. Do you feel the same way?"

"Yes! We are both old souls who um… met again in this life time to finish something not done before." Anne responded.

"My sentiments exactly, and because of that realization, I believe we should tread these new waters gently and patiently without any rush."

Anne's eyes lit up while he continued, "We are destined to be together, and I personally will do whatever it takes to protect it and enjoy its path. It's the journey that um… we should look forward to, not the destination. I know we will get to where we want to go already. The key is to slowly figure out how to enjoy the walk with fun and lots of love… That is my Truth."

"Fredric my love, I can't get over how you have been transformed. Your new philosophy about life amazes and pleases me beyond description. Did I hear you say 'no rush'? Please elaborate." Anne was curious to know!

"Hear me please! I put myself in your shoes… you have spent a lifetime studying and building a successful practice. You--you cannot simply drop everything and run away to be with me. You have obligations and responsibilities towards your patients, your family and your friends. I—I cannot be selfish and insist that you should leave right away if I love you, I have to help you to be comfortable and at ease, with the steps you need to take to enjoy a smooth transition. I know I'd love to--to have you here tomorrow.

"But, we are not high school kids to make such demands. So, I want you to—to take all the time you need, and I mean all the time, be it months, a year, or whatever! Yes, I want you to be with me at the end, on my side with work, and primarily as my life partner. I'm truly, passionately, and deeply in love with you… But on your terms, not mine. That's what I mean by 'no rush'."

Freddie took a deep breath after his long passionate and spontaneous speech. Anne kept silent for a while, gazing at him in the eye and smiling. Then, all a sudden she started crying. She jumped out of her chair, sat in his lap and hugged him while still sobbing. She cooled down after a couple of minutes and said,

"You can't imagine how relieved I am now hearing you speak to me like that. You read my mind and a—a large brick has been lifted off my back. I hoped you'd be patient but your statement of truth and sincerity, leave me no choice but to make sure not to lose you. You are a rare breed and I love you very much… I admit I had a tough couple of weeks away from you, pondering your request for me to join you… But now, I appreciate your understanding of the work required of me um… before I make my move. I also would love to be here as soon as possible because I love your company, particularly now that you've become so mature, so wise and so romantic. I feel much better now. Thank you!" Anne responded in kind.

The two of them took a break from talking and continued to eat the food while it was warm. They laughed and giggled between bites, then Anne asked him what is it he said he wanted to show her during the visit.

Freddie replied,

"I'd like to show you two spaces tomorrow... One is an apartment for us, a home, to live in once you're ready and assuming you like it first. The other, is a beautiful office space of about 5000 sq. ft. to be used as headquarters for DAA... including a separate space for your private practice."

"Man you're efficient when did you find these spaces? This is New York after all..." Anne questioned

"The company owns them so we're lucky they'll be vacant soon."

"You mean you own them?" Anne asked.

"Well! Yes, now, my father added these two buildings to the company portfolio before he passed away." Freddie explained.

"Where will I live?" Anne quizzed teasingly.

"If you don't want us to live together, we have many other apartments um... for you to choose from." Freddie replied wondering why she asked.

"I'm kidding, don't take it so seriously. I would only live with you... you spoil me, and I love it." Anne said with a giggle.

"That's my girl! Now you're talking."

They finished eating then moved to the sofa with the ice bucket to sip on the champagne while relaxing after dinner. Anne looked at Freddie with warm piercing eyes and simply said "Thank you." He moved closer to her and kissed her passionately for a whole minute, and told her how much he missed her. She took off her bathrobe and her gorgeous sexy body ignited his fire and drew him even closer to hug and kiss every part of her body that he could reach. That lasted few more minutes before he excused himself to take a quick shower, when he heard her say, "I'll be waiting for you in bed". The rest of the evening was formidable, and full of love and affection. They later slept peacefully with their bodies intertwined as one.

***

The happy couple woke up around 9:00 am and prepared to leave around 10:15 after breakfast, for their first appointment to see the apartment.

On the way over Freddie showed her a map of Manhattan and how the streets are designed between Avenues in length and streets in width. Also he explained how the island has two sides, the east and the west. Central Park is in the middle of the island. They are arrived at the building, which he had not seen for more than three years. He was met by one of his managers and the architect in the vast lobby. Anne said,

"Wow, this is a high rise. Which floor are we going to?"

"The 23rd, you'll see. It's not the highest. There are more floors in the building, I guess."

They walked out of the elevator and turned right. They entered the space and Anne was in awe of the size and decoration of the place. She was taken by the all around terrace that showed the view of the river and Queens to the east, and the view of the midtown skyline to the west. The master bedroom was huge and so was the main living areas and dining connected to an open kitchen with a counter in between. She was dumbfounded and was silent throughout the tour.

She liked the furniture that looked brand new. The manager told her the nephew of the Sultan of Brunei had rented the apartment furnished it and never used it. Freddie told her she can change anything in the furniture or fixture and it will be redone according to her taste. She responded, "No it's fine. Thank God it is super modern and not Brunei style". They looked around for 15 minutes and then left to go see the office space.

Freddie asked her while in the car,

"So, did you like it?"

"I love it... I can see us living there for sure. It is a palace compared to my tiny place... Take it and move in as soon as you can. Enough with the hotel life! You can hire a maid and have food delivered to you if you want. The location is great too."

"I appreciate your approval... I will tell them in my office to register it in both our names. Okay?"

"Both our names? Are you serious? Why? You said it is yours already? This place is worth more than $15 million in the market! Forget me, just put it in your name."

"No, it is ours… we have many other properties… It is my gift to you, um even if you decide you can't come… I don't care about the money. I want you to feel secure you have something in your name at least." Freddie reassured her trustfully.

Anne started sobbing again and she hugged him. Then with misty eyes said said, "thank you for trusting me already, and I adore you!"

They stepped out of the car in front of the town house. Anne asked, "Here? This gorgeous townhouse for an office, Wow!"

They walked in and she was astounded by the vast space of the first floor. She visited every floor while the architect was making suggestions to how the executive rooms will be designed and the large space for employees. When they reached to top floor,which consisted of a separate apartment complete with a kitchen, a large room and a conference area and a bathroom, Freddie told Anne,

"This could be um… your private space to use, for your own work, if you like it. Otherwise, we have a lot of office spaces in the city to choose from."

Anne looked around and saw that there was a balcony attached to this well-lit space, with an angle view of Central Park and said,

"Sweetheart, this is wonderful… it's a dream come true!"

"Good… I'll ask them to re-touch it, furnish it and paint it with the color you like. The elevator makes it easier for your patients to visit as well." Freddie said in front of his colleagues to note.

The architect then asked if he's allowed some time, it would be great if he could have a staircase connecting the first and second floors to make it look more as an office. Freddie exchanged glances with Anne and said,

"OK, as long as it can be ready in about one month, not more."

The architect confirmed it could be done. Freddie then told them to get started as soon as possible and he will notify James the lawyer it will be the address for the organization.

Freddie then asked Anne if she would like to come with him to the office for less than an hour then they'll go for lunch nearby. Anne was delighted to join him and he gave the driver the address to take them there.

***

Every one working in his open office space froze to look at the stunning women walking next to their boss. Anne nodded to all those that were looking at her before they reached his corner office at the end.

"It's so good to see your work place, boss!" Anne said happily.

"That's were I make my living... thanks for coming with me."

His assistant walked in and he introduced her to Anne and said,

Anne this is Laura my private assistant. If for whatever reason you cannot find me she'll know where to reach me. Laura said, "It's a pleasure to meet you Anne. Freddie thinks the world of you... Here is my business card with all my numbers. Call me... if you ever need any help." Then she looked at her boss and said,

"I'm still receiving requests for more interviews. You told me to say no, and I did. Is that still OK?"

"Yea fine ... fine, no more please."

Before Laura walked out of his office, she looked back and said,

"Sorry to bother you Anne, many people who saw you walking in are wondering which movie you acted, and asked me if you could sign their autographs."

Both Freddie and Anne laughed out loud and Anne asked Freddie, how big is the staff. Laura answered, "we're about twenty." Then Anne told Laura, "come with me and I'll go out and shake their hands and tell them I'm a simple women. Is it OK darling?"

Freddie smiled and told her, "go ahead be my guest... and that's sweet of you!"

Anne walked out with Laura who introduced her as Dr. Stevenson. Anne stopped at every desk and introduced herself as Freddie's girl friend and wished them a good day. Some asked her to sign an autograph, she held back and said, "I'm just a simple woman". Ten minutes later, she walked back to his office and said,

"That's it... they told me I should replace you, they're not happy with your management style. So, move over tiger!"

Freddie looked at her and burst out laughing. They both did. He then said,

"You're welcome to take my place anytime... I'm sure they adore you already for your humble gesture!"

"Humble indeed! I'm a genuine Midwest American… People love that, it's rare to find someone like me in a big city like this, don't you think?" Anne said jokingly.

"Absolutely correct… you are a gem and it's written all over your beautiful face." Freddie said affirmatively.

"OK, go ahead with your work… and I won't disturb you anymore. May I use your conference room? I need to call my office and see how my substitute analyst is doing?"

"Please go ahead and, I'll ask Laura to get you a nice cup of coffee," Freddie said.

"Aren't you sweet?"

Half an hour later, Freddie said, "OK, let's go! It's lunch time."

They walked out, and suddenly they saw the staff standing in ovation, clapping their hands and cheering the lovely couple. Anne waved at them with a big smile of gratitude.

***

During the short walk over to the restaurant James called Freddie to and said. " I met with Judge Lumen in his chambers and discussed the early release of Jane. He was favorable to the idea and asked me to fill out an application, as an official request. So I'm working on it and will let you know what develops."

"Thanks, James."

When they were seated at the table Freddie told Anne,

"That was James my lawyer on the phone. He met with the judge who sentenced Jane to three years in Jail. I asked him to check if we can reduce her sentence. And …instead of paying me money as per the sentence, she could work pro bono for DAA. She can be a witness to—to all participating women advising them not to do what she did. Eventually she'll be working for you. And I hope you are OK with that."

"What a benevolent man you are Fredric… This is unbelievable. Forgive and forget! You are a noble man indeed. Of course I bless it, and God Bless you. What did the judge say?"

"More or less what you just said… he's working on it. You know Anne I am cleansing my soul. I don't have an iota of anger or vengeance left in me. To forgive is to heal one's own soul." Freddie said eloquently.

"I love you!"

"I love you more!"

They both smiled and went on with their lunch order. Freddie then told Anne,

"I forgot to tell you that I had a surprise visit in my office from my ex wife, Matilda on Monday. She came in peace to tell me that she's seeing another man, a medical doctor in the same town She asked for my blessing and added how happy the boys were when they spent the last weekend with me last weekend."

"That sounds wonderful. There's nothing like a peaceful relationship between parents… for the sake of the kids also. I don't have this with my ex… and thank God there were no kids to complicate it further." Anne affirmed.

"Also to complete the gossip circle, Barry and Melody are getting married soon… may be we should have dinner together this weekend." Freddie added.

"I would love to see them again, and are you the best man?"

"What do you think? Of course I am… otherwise no marriage." Freddie said jokingly. Then he continued with another question,

"How do you feel about being here and from what you've seen so far?"

"I'm happy I decided to come, I feel so at peace with you around. I want to cuddle with you and hug you all the time. Mostly, I love listening to you… you've become such a wise man. Wow! I am looking forward to— to eventually move here. I appreciate your patience and your willingness to wait until I sort out my stuff back home. We need to figure out how to see each other more frequently, in the interim period." Anne explained.

"I thought about that. How about if we see each other every other weekend. We take turns. One time you fly in… and another time I fly over to be with you. How does that sound? We make Friday through Monday." Freddie suggested.

"It sounds reasonable… but costly." Anne said.

"Hey… I don't want to hear that again. All tickets are on me please… And since you're talking about money we need to discuss your compensation package at DAA… I take it you're doing very well now, and you should be paid um… at least the net yearly income you generate now. Besides, you will continue to have your own income from your private practice as it grows." Freddie assured her.

"Sweetheart you are being very generous. Let me think about that… we have time. Let's spend a jolly good time together now, and I have no concern about other mundane matters… all I want is our happiness and the success of our future journey together." Anne said.

"Do you want to meet my mother?" Freddie asked abruptly.

"What? Did I hear you right? Visit your mother? Are you on good terms now?" Anne asked.

"We talk few times a year… I want to introduce you to her, more as a formality and a good gesture to try and be warm to her."

"That's is a good idea. It's evident that you have forgiven her negligence during your childhood. Where does she live?"

"Still in her mansion in Greenwich Connecticut… where else!"

"So go ahead and plan it… I look forward to meet her." Anne emphasized.

"OK I will, and it seems we're going to have a busy weekend. I'll also drive you around in the country… it's lovely up there." Freddie said joyfully.

They finished their meal and went to the hotel to get some rest.

CHAPTER 12

Continued Affirmations

Freddie called me to say that Anne is in town and invited Melody and me to Dinner on Saturday. Then he called his mother who was happily surprised he called, and asked if he could see her tomorrow around lunchtime. He told her he would like to introduce her to his new girl friend. She was delighted to hear, and she said she would cancel her other engagements. She insisted that lunch would be served at home.

He later called Laura to tell her to prepare his car in the garage, to be at his hotel at 11:00 am.

"I didn't know you have a car!" Anne asked.

"I rarely use it except on weekends sometimes." Freddie replied.

"That was a good nap, do you have a coffee machine by the way? Anne wondered.

"Only espresso! If you prefer percolated coffee we can order."

"No, espresso is fine. It's in the small kitchenette right?"

"Right... my dear! Let me do it for you..." Freddie offered

"No, stay where you are I'll find it." Anne smiled and walked over to the small kitchenette and said,

"Wow... it's complete with everything, even a stove, good! I'll cook dinner for you tonight."

Freddie couldn't help but laugh and said, "you know how to cook my doctor friend?"

"You bet I do... I'm not a spoiled brat! I'm from the Midwest, a genuine American. I know how to fry eggs also... do you want an espresso my spoiled New Yorker?" Anne asked gleefully.

"Yes please, my adorable egg cook." Freddie replied while he uttered quietly to himself "thank God for restaurants, or else I might starve."

"I heard that! Keep talking to yourself, and I will only cook for myself... fine!" Anne pretended to be upset.

Then she walked out with two small cups of coffee with some biscuits she found. She told Freddie, "and the biscuits are for me only."

"I love it when you are in such a good mood. You look more beautiful and sexy!" Freddie said while watching her put the coffee cups on the table and run towards him asking for a hug. While sitting in his lap she said,

"Let's go for a walk in the Park after coffee... I want to remember our first walk together too."

"Consider it done, and we can sit on the same bench when we first met..." Freddie said romantically.

"Can we afterwards have dinner at the same restaurant you took me, near the Central Park entrance?" Anne asked

"Sure! Let me call Cipriani and reserve a table at seven."

They spent an hour and a half walking in the park, hand in hand, and enjoying the cooler breeze of the day. Before turning back they also found the same bench, and sat there for 15 minutes, giggling and mimicking joyfully the scene when they first met.

At the dinner table, Freddie asked Anne,

"Do you have a specific plan for turning over your practice?"

"Not, not yet! I needed to come see you first, to—to be re-assured that I am making the right decision. I'll start the process when I go back, now that I'm definitely decided to be with you, my love!" Anne replied.

"Good to hear! How do you normally go about it, in your business?"

"Either by an ad in the local papers, or through an agent, or by word of mouth among colleagues... Something, or someone will show up. Then the negotiation starts about the transfer cost to the new practitioner... I'll be very reasonable." Anne explained.

"In the unlikely event no one shows any interest. What do you do?" Freddie asked curiously.

"It is very unlikely, as you said, because I have a strong list of patients who live in the area, and my location suits them. However, if after a certain time nothing bites I will shut it down... and send letters of apology to my patients." Anne said affirmatively.

"That's a good plan! And I am certain your patients will eventually miss you. Let's wait it out and see... I hope you get what you will be asking for. Later, when you start here, and it may take a while, but you will attract many new patients, I'm sure." Freddie said confidently.

"If my eventual practice grows fast, how do you expect me to continue with the added responsibility um… you're giving me as CEO of DAA?" Anne rightfully asked.

"I thought about that, and it could happen, in the beginning however, your main focus will be to—to organize and run DAA. You will hire capable assistants, and slowly delegate the running of the operation to um… the most promising one. As such, you would eventually turn over a big part of your work to that person. That's what I do with my work. You will continue to be the CEO nevertheless, while your practice is growing. No one that I know has your expertise, education and amazing personality. Agree?" Freddie

"No wonder you're such a successful businessman… I agree! By the way, why should I be paid a salary um when I will be living with you for free, and… hopefully earn more money from the practice?" Anne asked.

"Sweetheart, I told you from the beginning that there will be a salary, in line with your current income… If you later receive big income form your own work um… you can reduce your salary from DAA proportionally. You're the boss, you decide! Please let's not discuss this any more, my love!" Freddie stated elaborately.

"God you're so generous… and God bless us with great success! I'm really excited by doing something very special with DAA. It's a great challenge! but we can do it." Anne said confidently.

"There will also be a board of directors and I would like you, James and Barry to be on the board… I'll be the chairman but without any executive power. We may later add um… two more members. I'm very excited too. Let's keep our fingers crossed!" Freddie stated.

"Let's drink to that…" Anne lifted her glass of wine and said it.

***

After a joyful evening and a relaxing night they slept comfortably in each other's arms and took their time to wake up and prepare for the drive out to see Freddie's mother. They took the elevator down around 11:00 am and his car was waiting outside.

"Is that yours, a sports car? Are we going racing?" Anne asked.

"Well that's what I have, I trust you can still fit in... with your sexy short skirt and long legs." Freddie commented.

"You're not that short either... smart man! I love this car, what is it?" Anne was curious to know.

"It's a Mercedes AMG GT. Would you like to drive it?"

"Are you kidding me? Why would you trust me?" Anne asked.

"Of course I do... I tell you what I'll let you drive it on the highway. It'll be easier and more fun. OK?" Freddie said.

"OK... I'm nervous, but I will."

Freddie pulled over after taking the exit to the highway and changed seats with Anne. He took a minute to explain how easy it is to drive. The gear was automatic and that made simpler for her. She adjusted her seat and took off. Freddie told her to relax and not to be afraid to go faster. She did, and started shouting from the thrill of the takeoff speed. He told her she's a good driver and as they got closer he pointed to the exit towards Greenwich. He insisted that she continues to drive all the way to the house.

Freddie asked her to pull up to the side of the big black gate 200 feet away, next to the buzzer. Anne remained silent while looking ahead at a huge residence, Mediterranean style. He told her his father built it 35 years ago and it is big. "I was the only child then, I don't understand why so big. It must have been my mother's idea because she loves to show off." Freddie said.

Anne entered the driveway when the gate opened and drove slowly, the long pathway with beautiful shrubs and flowers on each side, until she reached the circular part with a beautiful fountain in the middle. She stopped the car in front of the the main entrance. A big solid wood double door was opened by the butler. Freddie told her he grew up in that monstrous structure and was not so happy.

The butler saw Freddie and said,

"So good to see you again Mr. Rodman! Please follow me. I will notify Mrs. Rodman you are here."

"Thank you Charles, how have you been?"

"Fine indeed, Sir!" Charles said with a British accent.

Anne was getting dizzy looking at the high-decorated ceiling over the vast shinning marble hallway that led to the library on the right and the main living area on the left. She noticed the two winding staircases that lead to the upper floors. Freddie held her hand and they sat on a stunning sofa in the impressive library. The butler asked them what they would like to drink, and they both said, "water please" at the same time.

Few minutes later, Freddie's mother, Mary walked in. They both stood up and Freddie kissed his mother on her cheek and then introduced Anne. Mary looked at Anne from top to toe and said,

"Wow Freddie! where have you been hiding this beauty? You look gorgeous my dear!" Mary said while still looking at Anne.

"Anne is my dear girl friend, and she's visiting from Madison, Wisconsin for the weekend… She's a Psychoanalyst with a doctorate degree in psychology. I met her um… few weeks ago, and we hit it off well. How are you doing, Mother?"

"I'm fine… fine, busy as usual. I am so proud of what you're doing Freddie… All Greenwich congratulated me for having such a wonderful humanitarian son. You are a celebrity in town now!"

Mary Rodman was an elegant older woman in her mid sixties. She carried herself gracefully with a flare of grandeur. She was known in town for her beauty, charitable contributions and membership in various social clubs. Her physical looks and shape accentuated her attractive presence in society. At 5ft. 8in. she was considered tall. Her slim body was also blessed with a gentle and harmonious face with piercing blue eyes, dainty nose and blond hair down to her shoulders. She was always well groomed and well dressed.

"You have such a beautiful home Mrs. Rodman… And thank you for having us here." Anne said.

"Please call me Mary otherwise I'll be obliged to call you Dr. …."

"Stevenson" Freddie completed the name. Then she continued,

"This is Freddie's home too… I promised his father I will pass it on to Freddie when I pass away."

"Mom you'll live a long life… and you can do with it whatever you like, you don't have to save it for me. Thanks anyway." Freddie said.

"I hope I can see you more often my son! Anne, please make sure that he does. I miss seeing him, and you seem to be a very lovely woman… and I'd love to see you too." Mary said.

"Thank you Mary! I'm sure that Fredric would want to--to do that, now that he has me to encourage him… and to also bring his two boys to see you too. Right Fredric?" Anne spoke gently.

"Right, my dear, your wish is my command!" Freddie uttered and they all smiled.

The butler walked in and announced that lunch is ready. They all stood up and walked over to the outstanding dining room with a table that easily seats 12 people. A well-dressed headwaiter pulled the chair for Anne to sit, while the butler did the same to Mary at the head of the table. Anne noticed that Freddie was not comfortable with this charade but managed to stay quiet. Another waitress walked in with a tray from the kitchen, followed by another waiter with another tray. Wine was offered and the visitors agreed to drink one glass each.

Freddie seized the moment to explain to his mother the plans for DAA, and the fact that Anne will be running the show within short. He added that with Anne's experience and education she would surely succeed to lead the organization to help out many women. Mary congratulated both of them and asked,

"So Anne, you plan to move to Manhattan soon?"

"Yes, as soon as I turn over my practice to another psychoanalyst… It may take a while but eventually I'll be next to Fredric, whom I love and adore." Anne said proudly.

"Uh ha, I'm so happy to hear that… Freddie deserves to be with a woman like you. Thank God, he was lost for a while, and now he's found! Make sure you take good care of Anne, Freddie I mean Fredric, as Anne calls you… (I like that by the way, it indicates that you have been transformed into a new man now)." Mary said factually.

"Well good, I hope every one is happy with me now, the 'new man'!" Freddie said facetiously.

They all smiled and Mary motioned to the Butler and told him to serve the dessert and coffee in the living room.

They spent another 30 minutes chatting together, then Freddie asked Anne if she would like to see the gardens. She agreed and Mary told him to show her the rest of the house, including your old bedroom as well. Freddie held Anne's hand and walked around the house downstairs and upstairs before they stepped out to see the magnificent big gardens, the swimming pool and the tennis court in the distance. Anne was truly taken by the overall beauty of the mansion and warmly thanked Mary, before they left to drive around as Freddie promised.

***

Freddie drove on the way back, allowing Anne to enjoy the scenery of nature from the private roads he knew in the country. Freddie asked Anne what she thought of his mother's character. Anne quickly answered,

"She's somewhat insecure and um… hungry for family love, it is evident that her need to be recognized as a socialite is—is an escape from reality. Did she make any effort to see your kids before your divorce?" Anne commented.

"No, not really… as I mentioned earlier she was always pre-occupied with herself, and to be a big society figure, even when I was with still at home, and before my father died. How do you explain that?" Freddie asked.

"I can tell you from my observations of other similar situations, your mother um… has yet to experience self-love. She has become addicted to social recognition and attention from others. She has yet to discover who she really is. Look how you did it successfully, though you went through some suffering first… but you turned it around positively to discover self-love and self-realization. She hadn't experienced that like you did. Besides, even the passing of her husband did not shake her to be awakened… So, I don't know, but it's never too late."

"I love to hear you analyze people… I think my mother should definitely be your first patient." Freddie said.

"I'll try to befriend her first and ease her into a friendly relationship." Anne suggested.

"I'm sure she will… she liked you a lot. She would have never instructed me to take care of you if she didn't like you."

Freddie confirmed.

"Good! That helps. So let's go and rest a while before we go to dinner with Barry and Melody. I miss cuddling next to you my privileged boy. And before I forget, how can your mother manage living alone in that big mansion?" Anne asked.

"She has a staff of 9 people working for her including 2 gardeners and a personal driver. They've become her family... She loves to order them around and she can afford it too. My father left her a ton of money to stay in the mansion. He gave me the business and its properties. He was a good man, but she was the boss around." Freddie said.

"Are you satisfied he gave you the business... How big is it and are you comfortable managing it?" Anne asked.

"Of course I'm grateful to that... Sometimes I forget how big it is, but I--I believe it is hundreds of thousands of square feet, may be millions? My managers know all these details... I don't dwell too much on the size, and I keep investing by buying more property. What else can I do with the surplus cash the business generates?" Freddie explained.

Anne was taken by his modest reply. Other men would have boasted an extravagant show-off style of life. He never talked about his wealth when they met, or even later. She found out bit by bit, from what she had observed. Anne truly admired this humble characteristic in him. They went to the hotel suite and rested for an hour before meeting their friends.

***

Freddie had reserved a table at a French restaurant he knows I like, a walking distance for the hotel. As usual, punctual me, I was there few minutes earlier and they saw us already seated when they arrived. This time Melody and I looked attentively at Anne and whispered to each other how stunning she looked. They exchanged warm greetings and hugs before they sat down at a round table.

Freddie said that they went and visited his mother in Greenwich for lunch, and showed Anne some of the countryside as well. I asked Anne,

"What did you think of Mary? The mother of Jes... I mean this holy man here."

"She's definitely a nice lady who enjoys authority and a good life. We got along well together. I made it clear to hear that I love and adore her son, so she had no other choice but to accept me. I also encouraged Fredric to visit her with his kids more often. She definitely needs more love from her family." Anne explained.

"Thank you Anne for clarifying to her our intimate situation... She now knows the reality of our relationship. And if you ask me, she was mesmerized by you." Freddie elaborated.

"So, what's the latest between you guys? Moving forward, I hope?" I asked.

"You want to find out now, before champagne, my eager beaver?" Freddie shot his first dart at me.

"You don't have to answer, you can drink... Anne and I will talk without you." I responded.

"It must have been a while since the two of you have seen each other... you're at it again, huh?" Anne intercepted.

They all laughed and Freddie asked Anne to go ahead and tell them. "He'll believe you more than me, sweetheart! Meanwhile, I'll order the champagne."

"I enjoy being around you guys... you really are good friends. Now, and briefly, I—I came this weekend to re-assure myself that the love we have for one another is intact. And I'm pleased that Fredric would be patient with me, as I need some time before I physically move. I can tell you already um... we are moving towards having a happy and prosperous future together." Anne said.

"Congratulations! Though I really don't understand why you chose him? I'm sure you—you can find any man you want, so why him?" I said with a vicious smile on my face.

Freddie looked at him as felt like punch him on the shoulder. Instead, we all laughed it out, knowing that I have a bad sense of humor sometimes. Then I added,

"What can I say, Freddie brings out the worst in me... Sorry!"

"Fine, no champagne for you tonight! What happened? Did you have a tough week, and now you're here to pick on me?"

"OK... now, can we enjoy few moments of peace?" Melody said then added,

"Any idea Anne when you will be moving? The reason I ask because we are inviting you to our wedding."

"You can rest assured that I'll be at your wedding, regardless." Anne responded.

"Great… and by the way we decided to--to get married in exactly 10 weeks from today, on a Saturday as well, and Freddie, don't worry, Barry still loves you, and you're still the best man." Melody said. The champagne had been served and glasses filled, and Freddy gave his to me and said, "Congratulations, and I love you man!" They all clicked their glasses in good cheer. I then said,

"By the way Anne, and Fredric, if I may call you that, Melody cannot continue to work with me after we get married… So, and we discussed this, she'll be delighted to—to work with you guys at DAA. I highly recommend her, she--she has excellent organizational skills."

"Wonderful! Fredric and I will be delighted to have her as a part of our team, Thanks already."

They took few moments to choose and order their food. While waiting to be served, Freddie said,

"I showed Anne the apartment we're going to live in… yes, and goodbye hotel… I also showed her the office space for DAA and her own private practice. We both liked these two spaces and I asked my colleagues to prepare them for us."

"What locations?" I asked

"The apartment is on 53rd between first and second, and the office is a townhouse on 56th between Madison and fifth." Freddie answered.

"How did you find them so quickly?" I asked again

"My people found them in our company portfolio."

"You mean they are yours already? I see, that's wonderful, and when will they be ready?"

"The apartment in a couple of weeks, and the office in about one month." Freddie explained.

"What do you think of Freddie's plan for DAA and what role will you help him with?" I asked Anne.

"The DAA project is amazing! And what a great idea from this amazing man who shoved away his anger and revenge… Fredric offered me the job of CEO. He said he trusts that I'll do a good job. He also provided me with space on the top floor for my private practice… I'm excited about this now, to tell you the truth… I'm very grateful for his generous offer too." Anne said with a big smile gracing her face.

"Fredric huh.. I like calling him that… perhaps we should all call you Fredric from now on? It's an affirmation of your new state of being, and your benevolent attitude. I'm also happy to hear about your role Anne, as the CEO of DAA. Freddie, I mean Fredric, made the perfect decision. I'm also glad you will continue with your own practice. As we told you before, you already have um… two male patients sitting here at this table… We need your help! May be not Fredric, because you helped him heal already, but for sure me, right Melody?" I said.

"We all need help sometimes." Melody said.

"I'm truly looking forward to my future move… and to have a wonderful relationship with all of you. I believe this original concept of guiding and helping other women will succeed. Fredric and I are fully dedicated to its growth, and I also plan to open similar chapters in other cities of the country. New York is not the only place were women's rights are infringed upon in such a manner… It may not be lawyers who would do the ugly work necessarily. It could also be gangs and other underground organizations… We have a great challenge ahead." Anne said passionately.

"How big a staff do you think you'll need?" I asked.

"We haven't discussed that yet, but I think we should start with at least five: a capable manager of operations, a receptionist/office manager, an accountant and an executive assistant to Fredric and me. The space is big and we can easily accommodate twenty as we grow. Am I right, dear?"

"Yes you are right! And if we eventually outgrow the space, there is more available. Barry, I trust you agree to be a member of the board." Freddie asked.

"I will be honored my friend!" I assured him.

"If I may add, I also see us doing seminars, giving lectures, documentaries, raising funds and… appearing on social TV and media programs once the momentum is triggered, the inertia of our work will develop automatically… I feel it in my guts." Anne said enthused.

"Wow my love, you are truly passionate about the project… I'm so lucky to have you on my side. We should also have a great website and hire a publicist." Freddie stated.

We spent the rest of the evening talking about different matters of life, we giggled and laughed and we finished at 10:00 pm. Melody and I truly admire Anne and we wished her a safe trip back, and looked forward to seeing her soon. She told us that she would be coming at least once a month, as she will alternate with Fredric every two weekends.

***

Freddie and Anne decided to take it easy on Sunday and chill out in the hotel suite in the morning. Apart from the general chitchat they exchanged the subject of DAA came up again. Freddie said,

"You know my love! What you said um… about your future expansion plans for DAA beyond this city, thrilled me to--to no end. I am amazed how you eradicated my apprehension… I was concerned that I—I was putting a lot of pressure on you to run the organization… I am so relaxed now to see how wrong I was. On the contrary, you are so enthusiastic about it. Hum… What a divine honor I am being given from the heavens above. I can only say thank you, from the depth of my heart." Freddie said passionately.

"You're right… I am excited and dedicated to launch DAA's new rockets of knowledge and awareness, and send them to the farthest places of this world. To me, what you have created here is—is an unprecedented adventure that I—I always dreamt about as something unique, and with global purpose. In universal language, it is called the Law of Dharma… I see this as an opportunity to—to make this mission my life purpose, the reason why I'm here on earth." Anne responded truthfully.

"Wow! I bow down and I extend my salutation to you with my 'Namaste' posture. I greet the Divine in you, my true angel!" Freddie admitted.

"Now to talk some business while I am here, what do you think of Melody as um… an executive assistant to you and me, later? Anne asked.

"I don't know her well! But I trust Barry. He's a tough guy to work for, and very fussy about the quality of his team. She must be good. Besides, Barry wouldn't recommend her to us if—if he didn't think she'd be very good at her job… I would definitely hire her and I will consult with Barry about her compensation. She's not available right away anyhow." Freddie explained

"I agree! I have good feelings about her. She doesn't talk much but… she's not dumb either. Barry strikes me as someone who--who only surrounds himself with intelligent people… like you! so do it."

"I will also ask Laura, my executive assistant to--to interview other candidates for secretarial positions... Also she would work with our webmaster to do the DAA website, and she can find us a good publicist... to promote our message to the outside world. I hope all this would be in place before you come." Freddie said.

"How about Jane, once she's released? What could she do?" Anne asked.

"It'll be sometime before she's released... court procedures are slow... perhaps you would be in charge by then, and you decide if you even want her on board... The reason I thought about it is because she can be a good testimony to other women by—by encouraging them to stay away from um... temptations like the one she had". Freddie said.

"I hear you my sweet loving and forgiving hero." Anne responded.

"How about we grab a bite to eat? I'll also check what's going on at Guggenheim Museum? I will ask the concierge to recommend a good concert... or a musical in the evening?" Freddie suggested.

"That sounds great... let me get dressed and we go." Anne said happily.

They ended up going to the museum and to an evening concert at Avery Fisher Hall featuring two of Beethoven's symphonies no. 5 and no. 7. They ate a light supper after the concert, went to bed early. Anne took a 10:00 am flight back to Madison.

CHAPTER 13

A new Adventure

Before Anne returned to Madison on Monday, she spent some time with Freddie discussing the organization structure and the budget for DAA. They agreed to have three departments: Education and Training; Marketing and Outreach; Administrative and Accounting. Each department will have a manager. These executives are to be hired before the end of the first six months. The department heads will have a budget to work with and hire their own employees. The total number of employees should not exceed 20 in the first year.

Freddie and Anne also discussed fund raising. Initially they have to work with the publicist once the website is ready, and to print brochures explaining the work and its objective. They acknowledged that the initial $2 million in the account are adequate for the first year of operation to cover salaries and office furniture and fixtures. Though Freddie assured her that he will continue to guarantee the obligations from his own pocket, Anne said that they should focus on fund raising as well, not only for the sake of more money coming in, but also to slowly expand, and open branches in other major cities.

Anne shared her vision with Freddie, which was the visualization DAA becoming a Franchise, and a brand name that will attract many to participate in its growth. She said that she would make it her priority to see it grow, even if it means she discontinues her practice as a psychologist.

***

James told Freddie, two weeks later that the organization has been registered officially and all the permits to operate were in place. Freddie, Anne,

James and Barry were registered as members of the board of directors. Meanwhile, the architect and Freddie's manager were doing the work preparing the two spaces as desired. Freddie moved into the apartment 15 days after Anne's return, and the Office space work was half finished.

In the same two weeks Freddie had a formal interview with Melody and was very impressed by her resume. He offered her a job of executive assistant and she agreed. He advised her to give the two-weeks notice to the company, and find a replacement to help Barry. Freddie understood that Melody needs a whole week off before the wedding coming up in about seven weeks.

Laura found a good receptionist/office manager that would start working as soon as the space is ready in about two weeks. Laura also arranged meetings with showrooms for furniture and fixtures, and lined up office suppliers as well. She told Freddie that the website is being worked on but will only be complete once the space is furnished and has some people working.

Freddie asked James if there was any progress with the court about releasing Jane and the answer was 'not yet'.

***

As agreed, Freddie went to visit Anne in Madison for the weekend. His earlier weekend with his children went very well again, and he also managed to take them out dinner every Wednesday. He kept good communication with Matilda and they spoke once or twice a week discussing the affairs of their children.

It was the first time Freddie visits Madison. He was eager to see Anne in her own surroundings. Two weeks had passed since they were together. He arrived at the Madison airport at 7pm on Friday evening and planned to stay till Monday morning. Anne picked him up in her Prius and they were both thrilled with joy when they met. She drove to her place first before they went out to have dinner.

On her way she briefed Freddie on Madison,

"It's a city of about 250,000 people… It's known for its lakes, university and food. But mostly, it's known for its friendly people… We also brag about our beer, fish fry and brats. You may want to try these before you go back… Fall, is beautiful time of the year and you're here to enjoy. It has is a cold breeze but very refreshing. I will drive you around later to see nature around the 4 lakes… It's so good to see you here, my love!"

"I'm so happy I came. It's so nice to be in 'your' America! This seems to be a lovely city. I look forward to my future visits. Do your parents live here as well?" Freddie asked.

"Yes, They do and I told them about us… they'd like to meet you. I said I'd ask you first."

"I would love to meet them. I want to see wherefrom you got your gorgeous looks. What do they do? Freddie asked.

"They are both University professors… My Dad teaches business ethics and my Mom teaches history. Both are proud of their Doctorate degrees as well." Anne said smiling.

"Wow, a family of doctors! Where do I fit in?" Freddie asked.

"In my heart!" Anne's answered quickly.

"Umm… that sounds so warm and delicious. Keep me there!"

They entered Anne's apartment and Freddie was shown the small three rooms that were neatly and beautifully decorated. He took a quick shower got dressed and said,

'Let's go for beer and brats!'

"You must be kidding… I already reserved a table at one of the best French restaurant in town, and I want to impress you!" Anne said not knowing if he was serious.

"That's great, I was kidding. You—you always impress me and I'll leave the sausages and beer for lunch tomorrow, OK?" Freddie said and hugged her.

"So tonight, we eat at L'etoile, and I'm sure you'll like it. I don't go there a lot it's expensive… I figured I'll take advantage of you being here and make you poorer! I'm joking, dinner is on me, in keeping with our tradition." Anne explained.

"I'm honored… Please let me pay for coffee at least." Freddie joked.

"We'll see, it depends on what kind of wine we drink. After, we can go listen to-to some jazz at café Coda if you like." Anne said.

"It's going to be a great evening, let's go!"

The restaurant was a cozy and romantic place that served very good food. After the main course, Freddie asked her,

"Is your ex still bothering you?"

"No, not anymore… He got the message and he's looking elsewhere, thank goodness!" Anne replied.

"How's you other friend, is she happy with her new boy friend." Freddie continued with his questions.

"Lara, her name, she's very happy and they plan to get married soon. We still talk couple times a week, and… I saw them both once since I got back from New York." Anne said.

"Any progress on your practice transfer?"

"Some… not a lot. Two guys expressed interest and I'm yet to meet either one. They both said they'd call me back to me soon… I'm waiting, while continuing to send the word out." Anne responded.

"An idea! Did you ask your friend Lara to take it over? Freddie wondered.

"No not really! First, she's afraid to take a chance, and she thinks I'm targeting a lot of money which she can't afford." Anne said.

"That sounds silly, if I may say! Her new boy friend should encourage her too… and you please tell her to—to pay you what she can afford. She's from the same neighborhood, and she knows many of your patients… I would call her again and encourage her to consider." Freddie attested strongly."

"OK sweetheart I will. Would you like to meet them, and help me out?" Anne beseeched.

"Fine, I'll do it. Let's meet them!" Freddie confirmed.

"I love you! You're a brilliant businessman. Anne said thankfully.

They went to Café Coda for some jazz music after dinner. They spent an hour and then went back to Anne's home around midnight. Their close presence together ignited their physical desire, and they demonstarted their love passionately before they went to sleep.

***

Anne called her parents in the morning and told them they would come to visit around 11:00 am. Both parents were eager to meet Freddie. The drive to their house took only 15 minutes and both parents were sitting out on the porch with blankets over their swinging chairs. They stood up when Anne pulled up and were first greeted by a healthy looking German

Shepherd dog. Both parents looked tall and very good-looking. Freddie immediately noticed where Anne got her beauty from.

Anne introduced Freddie, as Fredric Rodman, and then said,

"This is my mother, Lisa and my Dad, Bjorn." She hugged them both and they all went inside for some coffee. The conversation was cordial and general talking about university teaching and New York life. Bjorn the father recommended that Fredric should see the University campus and asked Anne to show it to him. Bjorn was about 63 years old and in great shape. He had white blond hair and a typical handsome Swedish face. He's about 6ft.2in. and he loves to watch American football and tennis.

Lisa walked out with the coffee from the kitchen together with Anne, who was told how gorgeous 'this Fredric looks'. Lisa was also 5ft.9in tall about the same height as Anne and they looked like twin sisters. Anne seemed to have a very healthy relationship with her parents. After all she was the only child, just like Freddie. They sipped the coffee and Lisa said,

"Anne is—is excited about her move to New York! We will miss her very much, all her friends and patients too." Lisa said

"Anne has a vision to reach out to the global community… and empower women to—to live a dignified life. I'm looking forward to be by her side to see her dreams fulfilled. I'm just a—a facilitator who will enjoy the manifestation of her ideas unfold into reality." Freddie said.

"You see Mom and Dad, I told you… Fredric is a philosophical poet who is humble to admit that he—he is the genius behind our future project. He's also a romantic poet. Hum… He's the one who wrote the poet I forwarded to you." Anne said proudly.

"Let's not exaggerate Anne, Please!" Freddie responded.

"What prompted you to be in the real estate business?" Bjorn asked.

"I inherited it from my father who's no longer with us… I'm lucky I guess!" Freddie said humbly.

"Fredric is a real estate tycoon… and owns many residential and commercial properties. He doesn't like to talk about it. He chose for us one of the most beautiful apartments I've ever seen." Anne bragged.

"I hope you'll come and visit us… We have a guest room for you as well. Anne's new home is yours too." Freddie said warmly.

"Fredric registered the apartment in both our names... I am so grateful for his trust in me already. I—I love him so much!" Anne responded with misty eyes.

"We wish you both the best of happiness and success... and Fredric it has been a great pleasure to know you. How about I take you to a Madison treat for lunch downtown, Bratwurst and beer?" Bjorn suggested.

"That sounds great, Anne told me about the brats."

The four of them went downtown and they proudly introduced Freddie to their city and a hint of their culture. Anne brought her parents back home and continued to show Freddie other landmarks and the four lakes Madison is known for. They also passed by the University campus where Anne graduated from.

***

While driving around in the car, Freddie reminded Anne to call Lara to discuss the transfer of her business. They stopped for coffee at a cozy café near the lake and Anne called Lara. She told her that Fredric is in town and she would like to introduce him to her, and her fiancé, John. Lara said they're free in the evening. Freddie told Anne to invite them to dinner at a restaurant of their choice. Anne put Lara on hold and asked Freddie if he likes to have a good steak and he quickly agreed. Anne then told Lara "let's meet at Tornado Steak house at 7:30 pm".

Lara was also a therapist like Anne, a pretty tall woman with auburn short hair and attractive features all around. Her soft brown eyes expressed her sweet personality. Though she preferred to work with a group it became a challenge to convince her to go on her own. That was an easy task for Freddie, a good negotiator and persuader. John sat there listening, as he knew very little about the practice. He worked as an investment banker. After eating their main courses, and drinking some wine, they felt comfortable in each other's company. And then Freddie looked at Lara and asked her,

"You and Anne are best friends and um... I'm sure she told you that she'd be joining me in New York in the near future. She will run the new organization we just established, and we will live together. You are also aware that she would like to transfer her practice to a trusted person... I asked her if she had discussed passing on her charts to you. Her answer was 'not yet'... Being the bashful person she is, I--I offered to raise this request on her behalf. So what do you think?"

"Wow... that would be a great honor. Anne has built an incredibly successful practice. Her patients adore her. I don't know if any one can fill her shoes... I've never been on my own before and I'm a bit apprehensive about it. Additionally, and truthfully her charts are priceless in value... I don't think I can afford it. Wow... I'm very happy you too are together and I'll miss her very much, so..."

Freddie interrupted her and said,

"Listen to me Lara, I believe this is your chance to prove to yourself how great you are, to take a chance! You're as good a psychoanalyst, as Anne at least that's what she told me. Just trust in yourself and put it in your mind that you'll succeed, and you—you will. When my father left me his business, I had no idea how to run it, but I trusted myself... and God blessed. Look at what Anne did, she trusted herself and she succeeded. You can do the same!

"Now, about the value of her charts, I agree with you that her list of dedicated patients is priceless... They are mostly from this area and you—you already know many of them. Imagine how they will respond positively um... when Anne notifies them that she's transferring the work to you, her best friend... This is a small town and they all know you two are friends. So that is not an issue. Now, about the money I talked to Anne, and we agreed that you—you offer her what you can afford. And, if you cannot afford to—to give her a symbolic amount, don't worry about it... Consider it a gift from both of us. Are you with me Anne on this one?"

Freddie concluded his presentation with confidence. There was silence on Lara's part for few seconds, Anne then intercepted Lara's deep thoughts and said,

"Lara, I am privileged to be with this man who is providing me with all the comfort I dreamed about... It will be an honor for me to pass on my practice to you. I—I believe in you and it would make me very happy to know you are taking it over. We are friends, and that's what friendship is all about. The value of my charts becomes priceless only if you take it. I don't want any money form you please accept. And we will have a smooth transition to turn it over to you. I—I really would like to join Fredric in the big city as soon as possible… Please think about it, and I'm certain John will support you also. OK?" Anne said passionately.

Lara stood up and went over to hug and thank both Anne and Freddie. With misty eyes she said,

"I am so lucky to receive this honorable gesture, and I will sleep on it tonight and um… will let you know in the morning. OK?"

"Fantastic, let's drink to Lara's divine guidance!" Freddie said. They all agreed no more business to discuss and proceeded to the jazz café again. Freddie liked it the night before. They joked and laughed and appreciated Freddie's good sense of humor and relaxed demeanor. Lara fully understood why Anne was in love with him.

***

As soon as Anne got in the car to drive home, she couldn't wait to tell him,

"You never stop to amaze me with how great you are… what you told Lara and… and how you explained the entire situation to her, will leave her no choice, but to agree. Thank you, my love." Anne said.

"I hope I did not upset you by speaking on your behalf regarding the money. I know that you—you know how much it is worth. Please give me the number, and I'll put it in your account on Monday. I just thought she was the right person to—to carry on with what you started." Freddie said sincerely.

"Fredric, on the contrary, I—I am very happy about what you offered on my behalf. Besides, I don't need to receive any money from you, on her behalf either… I feel very secure with you. You made me very rich already. Your overwhelming generosity and love is what is priceless to me… Let's keep our fingers crossed that she will agree to take it by tomorrow… With Lara, the transfer will be smooth and short." Anne said gratefully.

They had a comfortable night in each other's arms, and slept peacefully.

***

The next day Lara called Anne around 10:00 in the morning. She said,

"I don't know um… where you found this man he—he is a rare gem. Both John and I thought of him as an angelic prophet… I congratulate you, and I wish you both the best of life. Fredric was not only a super salesman last night, but was like a voice from heaven encouraging me to take a chance on life… and to become an entrepreneur like you. I—I am embarrassed about the money part though.

"What I can do sweet Anne is to—to pay you 20% share of my income every year for five years… I'm sorry I don't have any cash to advance you. If this is not workable, I also understand… Our friendship is extremely valuable to me, and I want us to be friends for life. So, that's my response, what do you think?"

"Lara, this is more than enough for me… Welcome on board! And as of tomorrow, we can meet after work and we'll go through the required steps for a—a smooth transfer of my practice to you. Feel free to submit your resignation soon and give the group the 2-weeks notice. I bet you within one month you'll be ready to—to start your own practice. Fredric will be extremely happy that you agreed. And, Yes we will be friends forever!" Anne reassured her.

"Thank you both very much and may the Universe reward you many times over. See you tomorrow around 6:00 pm and… hugs to Fredric from John and I." Lara said happily.

Anne and Freddie spend the rest of day relaxing and seeing some touristic attractions. Anne showed him the Wisconsin Capitol building, with its rising high with its impressive architecture between scenic Lake Monona and Lake Mendota. Then they went to Olbrich Botanical Gardens to enjoy nature and stroll the vast stunning landscapes of exotic plants and flowers, its trees, its glass pyramid the waterfall. Freddie truly enjoyed walking around for more than hour in this relaxing surrounding.

After an enjoyable lunch in town, Anne took Freddie to see another stunning architectural landmark, the Overture Center for the Arts in the midst of the Arts District in Madison. Anne stopped to check the performance scheduled for that evening. She found that The Madison Symphony Orchestra was featuring the cellist Zuill Bailey performing Elgar's cello concerto, and Tchaikovsky symphony no. 5 with Tania Miller as a visiting Canadian conductor. They agreed to finish the day with this promising performance and bought the tickets.

They had a chance to go home and change for the concert and have a light meal beforehand.

Freddie said goodbye on Monday morning and thanked Anne for a wonderful weekend and the fact he met her parents, her friend Lara and seeing the charming city.

CHAPTER 14

The Challenge Ahead

Freddie was in his office early afternoon and he was told that his apartment would be ready to move in before end of the week. The work on the office space is in progress and should be finished in about three weeks. His assistant Laura told him that she scheduled a meeting with a publicist the next day, and she asked the webmaster to start the work on the DAA website immediately. Laura already lined up the office furniture and fixtures to be delivered, once the space is ready.

Freddie called me from his office and told me how much he enjoyed his visit with Anne, and how he persuaded her friend Lara to take over her practice.

"So, this should not take Anne a long time to move, right?" I asked.

"I hope so, Anne says it would take less than a month now. She also said she will notify the landlord that she plans to vacate the apartment in one month. I—I would say she should be here in 4 to 5 weeks." Freddie said.

"That sounds good! She'll be here um… right when the office space will be ready. Are you happy?" I asked.

"Very happy! I tell you my friend, the more I spend time with her the more I—I love her. She's a very pleasant and intelligent woman… I also met her parents, two professors at the university of Wisconsin and… both tall and gorgeous looking. Are all the Swedes like that? I wonder!" Freddie expressed happily.

"Good to have you back and let's get together soon. Melody submitted her resignation today… and I—I asked her to hang around for two more weeks to find me a replacement. She's excited about working with Anne she really liked her. Once she frees herself up from here she'll help you set up the office too." I said.

"Thanks a lot Barry, I'm so happy to—to have you all in my life now… I'm experiencing joy and peace like I've never had before. What a change?" Freddie said.

Laura then walked in to say that The Center has made a request for Professional Responsibility, part of the American Bar Association. "They requested your agreement to be the keynote speaker during their upcoming annual conference here in the city six weeks from now." When I told them, "But… Mr. Rodman is not a lawyer."

The guy answered,

"We know that… we want our members to hear his unique story first hand and to officially apologize to him on behalf of the American Bar Association… The center monitors the discipline rules, and the behavior of all registered lawyers."

"So what would you like me to tell them?" Laura asked Freddie.

"Okay I'll do it! I will seize this opportunity to promote DAA and ask them to donate… How about that?" Freddie emphasized.

"You're a genius, Boss! How was your weekend with gorgeous Anne? We all love her here, I want you to know!" Laura said.

"Good… very good… Can we go back to work now?" Freddie demanded.

Freddie called Laura again and asked her to make sure the apartment is ready by Friday afternoon, as he wants the kids to be with him the first weekend. Once confirmed, he asked her to also settle with the hotel and arrange for his belongings to move to the apartment. Laura confirmed an hour later that all is set for the move.

She also showed him clippings of all the write-ups about him in the media journals and magazines. She had all the cuttings neatly organized in a nice file. Freddie didn't want to go through it and moved it aside. He told Laura,

"I appreciate you doing this, but I—I don't really care about getting recognized or famous… I just want to focus on the challenge ahead. Thanks anyhow!" Freddie stated.

James called him in the afternoon to say that the judge will meet with him on Wednesday in his chambers to discuss the process of Jane's earlier release and a document has to be signed on your behalf agreeing to this request. Freddie then told him about the invitation by the Bar association to be a keynote speaker during the conference. James was happy to hear about that and confirmed that he and three other lawyers from his firm will be there. He added that there will around 2000 lawyers attending this conference, and it's a great exposure for DAA.

Freddie informed James that Anne should be arriving in about one month and we should have the first board meeting shortly thereafter.

Later in the evening Freddie spoke to Anne who briefed him on the first meeting with Lara and she said,

"First let me tell you Fredric, Lara is so happy for us and she was really taken by your caring personality… She's excited about the transfer and I—I assured her again it would be smooth. We are arranging for the legal part of the transfer as well. I showed her the list of patients I treat and she knew few of them. I explained the hourly charges per session, and how to keep the books in order… I told her that as of tomorrow I'd start writing personal letters to—to the dozens of clients I have, and explain the reasons for the transfer… I will reassure them how good Lara is."

"I'm very glad to hear that and I wish her the best of luck! Laura here has been working diligently to get the apartment ready this week and the office should be operational by the time you're with us. I'll be with the boys this weekend… and hopefully their room would be ready at the apartment. I can't wait to have you—you, next to me in our bedroom." Freddie said.

"I miss you already and I'm so happy you came. My parents adore you… They normally don't express their feelings about someone they meet the first time. But um… they broke their cold Swedish tradition in your honor, my love." Anne said happily.

"I like them too. I am invited by the American Bar Association to—to give a speech during their national conference here in New York, six weeks from now… and I accepted. This would be a good time to promote DAA. I hope you'd be here by then, um… to share it with me." Freddie said.

"Hum mm… that sounds great Sweetheart. It must a large conference, and I'm sure… they chose you to coach their lawyers how to conduct their business ethically." Anne said.

"James told me to expect around 2000 conferees. And I will challenge them to donate to DAA. So please—please come and share the stage with me... you're the CEO! You can also speak about DAA. With you it'll be a smash hit and I guarantee you all the lawyers will donate a fortune to the organization... once they see the beautiful leader of DAA on stage... So, do we have a deal?" Freddie beseeched.

'My Love, I'm not used to speak in public, you do it." Anne said.

"No...No I insist. Don't you want DAA to succeed?"

"You're trying to convince me as—as you convinced Lara aren't you?" Anne asked.

"You're both Psychologists, and I understand your language by now... please say yes...please! Only 5 minutes on stage, may be 10 will see! OK?" Freddie asked.

"I'll think about it, and I will let you know tomorrow... How about that super salesman?"

"I thank you for accepting in advance. I look forward to your forthcoming confirmation first thing in the morning... we are at your service mam. Thank you again!" Freddie said with a hoarse voice.

"You—you! You're lucky I'm not next to you... to give you a nice punch in your tommy!" Anne said laughing.

"I love you, and have a great night!" Freddie said gleefully.

"I love you too... have sweet dreams!"

***

Freddie met with Dania, from a well-known Publicist agency in the city. Dania was already familiar with the story from the media but Freddie explained to her in more details his objective and what he intended to achieve. He told her about Anne the CEO of the organization. He emphasized that DAA should become a brand name and he asked Dania to give him a proposal explaining how the agency will proceed to induce companies and government agencies to donate.

He told her that the focus is on the tri-state area around New York, but eventually should go national. Dania assured him that they will be specific in what media outlets to recommend, and the quality of the website to include visuals and videos. She also said that there should be special invitations to black-tie gala dinners and parties. She told Freddie that she would come back with a detailed program, including the logo for DAA, within 3 weeks.

Freddie called James to ask him if he can recommend a good speechwriter to edit his message in the conference. James told him to write down what he wants to say, and his office will take care of the rest. James also liked the idea of Anne to give part of the speech to talk about the DAA organization.

Freddie informed Anne later that a speechwriter will write up her part as well, and all she needed to do was to write down the main points. She felt more at ease when she heard that and confirmed to 'Fredric' that she would be happy to participate.

I saw Freddie that evening for a drink after work. We discussed the speech to be given at the conference. And I also liked the idea of Anne speaking as CEO of DAA. I said,

"Anne, with her qualification and great looks will be a big hit."

"I told her so myself she was shy first, but then said yes… James said he would have a—a speechwriter edit the speeches for us. I also met with the publicist today. We should get a proposal from her agency in 3 weeks… So, things are moving well and I'm most excited um… about Anne coming sooner than I expected. She's currently turning over the practice to—to her best friend, Lara" Freddie said.

"You know Freddie, I have to say it. Three months ago I was worried about you… I don't want to talk about the past, but do you remember the dream you told me? You were really living on the dark side of the moon. Thank goodness you had the strength to leave Jane, guided to search within, and to meet Anne. You transformed to—to a completely different person now. You're actually enjoying the bright side of the moon …and hopefully sunlight forever. I'm so happy for you! It was a wake up call, and you—you turned the past suffering and despair into peace and joy… You deserve to be happy, please enjoy every moment." I said sincerely.

"Thanks Barry, my life is so much better now. I am grateful to—to the inner guidance I received and believed. And I am particularly grateful to you and Anne… for being there for me when I needed you." Freddie responded with compassion.

"I can't get over God's gift to you. I mean—Anne. The two of you are such a great couple… and your plans will definitely bear good fruit. How she's going to manage her own practice, and run DAA is going to be a big challenge, but she'll pull it through." I said.

"She told me she was willing to—to give up her private practice if DAA needs her more." Freddie said.

"Wow! She's really dedicated to helping others, in a global way. This could be more satisfying to her than her current career … Besides, I'm sure you'll take very good care of her financial needs." I said, while standing up to leave.

"Thanks for coming Barry… I will take care of Anne, no worries." Freddie said before each went in a different direction.

***

Freddie called Anne when he got home. She had just finished another session with Lara and the transfer process was going well. Lara also agreed to a copy of the letter Anne intended to send to her clients announcing the transfer. Then she added,

"Love, you said James will help us find a speechwriter, and I thought, why look far, my father is… a professor on Ethics. Perhaps he can help?"

"It wouldn't hurt to ask him! … You can discuss with him your part and I will see what James can do for my part… We have time to exchange ideas that transpire between us… Barry says hi, we just had a drink together. Melody will be available to help us out in two weeks. How was your day?" Freddie asked.

"It was a productive day… I'm beginning to notify the clients I see, about the new change and they wish me well. I'm sending letters out to the others, and I think it will go smoothly… I should be able to with you within short." Anne said.

"I can't wait! I'll be with the boys this weekend, as you know. Your turn to—to visit will be the weekend after. Please give me your itinerary to book the tickets." Freddie advised.

"Sweetheart… I have money please relax! I had a successful career, remember? I appreciate your gesture… but I ask you to please let me take care of my travel I wish I am with you now, OK?"

"Fine my love, do what makes you feel better… soon we will be together, I'm so excited. With you on my side I—I truly feel more empowered and enthused about the challenges waiting for us. Barry told me that we are bound to succeed together… It's the power of two." Freddie said.

"I share his opinion! I believe we are destined to be together. And we have similar dreams about what we want to accomplish. We are both intelligently aware and dedicated to the cause. Hence, we are bound to see all our wishes fulfilled." Anne explained.

"I am with you all the way, dearest Anne. I am blessed and grateful to the divine power that guided me to—to sit next to you on that bench in the park… I wish I could buy it to keep it as a souvenir." Freddie wished gleefully.

"It is a beautiful destiny and a wonderful change of pace for me. Do you think I planned, or knew that I—I would be living in New York and not work in Madison? That thought never crossed my mind couple of months ago… The Universal Law of Attraction is what brought us together. We ask, we believe and we receive. We both believe in what we want, and for sure the universe will give it to us." Anne said beautifully.

"The challenge is to—to be persevere, looking ahead and leaving the past behind us. With your wisdom and understanding of people and with my spiritual ambition and business experience, I am certain we will succeed with DAA… and happy working and living together… It's like a dream come true for me." Freddie said joyfully.

"Fine, my love, I am going find some food in the fridge to eat. I love you and wish you a good night… Until tomorrow, kisses!"

***

James called Freddie the next day and told him, "The judge says that a short hearing will be held in—in two days which will allow us an official request to—to reduce Jane's sentence in jail. I told him the request would be based um… on our finding out after the fact, that she was coerced and threatened to do what she did. She can be considered as a victim… not a villain, now that we know the truth that she worked under pressure from her lawyer."

"What do you expect he'll decide?" Freddie asked.

"It's just a guess on my part! He'll reduce the sentence between 6 months to one year… It's the closest thing to dropping the charges. Let's wait and see! Meanwhile, he instructed Mr. Padowski, the lawyer to execute the transfer to—to the DAA account within 48 hours."

"Noted, thanks! James, before you go, is it okay if Anne's father helps her to—to write her part of the speech? He's an ethics professor and knows this stuff well… and, did you have a chance to work on the deed for the apartment as we discussed?" Freddie asked.

"It is absolutely fine if her father can help out. We'll take a look at it anyhow. I have yet to follow through on the deed but I'll submit the request before the end of this week I promise!" James said.

"Okay thanks, and bye for now!"

***

Freddie spent the rest of the week paying attention to his real estate business. He spoke with Anne every evening and couple more times with Barry. He arranged with Matilda that he could pick up the kids on Friday evening to take them to the new apartment for the weekend. Matilda said she wouldn't mind dropping them off and take a look at the apartment if he doesn't mind. Freddie told her she's welcome to see it. This way she can visualize the children in their new home in the city.

The apartment was fully ready by 5 pm on Friday, thanks to the diligent work of Laura. She managed to have new sheets and pillows in all three rooms, a thorough cleaning job of all the rooms, and a maid to be there as of Monday morning. Matilda was given the address and she said she'd be there around 6 pm. Freddie was already waiting for them at the apartment.

The doorbell rang around 6 pm and Freddie opened the door. He hugged his kids first then gave Matilda a friendly hug. The boys were happy to see this big place, and Freddie invited Matilda to look around. He told the boys it is their choice to share the same room with two beds or sleep in two separate rooms. They loved the fact they did not have to share a sofa in the hotel anymore. Matilda was impressed with the place and was happy to see the boys excited about it.

"Would you like a cup of coffee?" Freddie asked Matilda.

"Yes please! Thank you."

They sat in the living room across from one another, while the kids were out sitting on balcony chairs and enjoying the distant views.

"When did you move in and how did you find this beautiful place?" Matilda asked.

"This is my first night here, I wanted to—to inaugurate it with the children first. The business owns the building, as you may know, and this apartment became available a week ago… It was furnished as you see it, by—by the nephew of the Sultan of Brunei, who never used it… So everything is brand new and looks okay." Freddie said.

"So, your girl friend is not here yet?" Matilda asked curiously.

"No not yet, she's still in Madison, turning over her practice and charts to—to a new psychoanalyst. Her name is Anne, and she might be ready to come in about a month." Freddie answered.

"I see, she's a psychologist? And will leave her work to move in with you?" Matilda asked wondered.

"That's the plan, also may be you don't know yet, she'll be the one running the non-profit organization I created, called DAA, or Dignity Above All. I'll be the chairman and she'll be the CEO." Freddie stated.

"Wow! You trust her that much already eh?" Matilda asked.

"You bet! May be you'll meet her one day… and you'll understand why she is a very capable leader… And so let me tell you the whole story in one shot… it will save you some questions. She's in her thirties, tall and beautiful, has a doctorate degree in psychoanalysis, and um… had her own practice for several years. I met her by chance few months ago, and we hit it off well. We love and respect one another now, and we—we share the same mission of reaching out to—to help young women make better choices for their lives." Freddie said politely.

"Thank you Freddie for the explanation and I truly wish you a happy relationship together… She sounds like a—a great lady. As far as I am concerned, everything is cool. John and I are still seeing each other, and the kids are comfortable with him around. I hope you'll meet him one day."

"By the way… perhaps I can take the boys for a drive to Greenwich to see their grandmother this weekend. She misses them a lot. Is that okay with you?" Freddie asked.

"No problem at all. I'll leave you now to be with the kids." Matilda stood up and said goodbye to the kids. Freddie thanked her for the visit and said he'll take the boys home Sunday evening.

Freddie had a great time with his boys all weekend. The decided to sleep in separate rooms. They saw a movie together in the living room.

They played monopoly and cards. They ate out twice and Laura had filled the fridge and pantry with food for breakfast.

Freddie explained to them that he has a new girl friend and she's a doctor of psychology and she'll be helping him to run the organization when she comes in about a month. They all laughed when Brian remarked, "Wow… both Mom and Dad have doctors in their lives now."

He also managed to drive them to see their grandmother on Sunday to get to know her better, and then dropped the boys off at home in Westchester county on his way back to the city.

***

Late on Sunday evening, Freddie received a call from Lisa, Anne's mother who told him calmly,

"Anne had to be admitted to the hospital unexpectedly on Saturday… due to some injuries that affected her right arm and hip… The doctors are optimistic she'll be okay soon."

Freddie asked her what happened and Lisa simply said,

"She had a fight with her ex-husband… He was drunk and broke into her apartment. She called 911 and the ambulance brought her to the hospital um… while the police went after her ex who is now behind bars."

"Can I talk to her?" Freddie asked Lisa, nervously.

"She is asleep now they gave her some pain killers."

"Please text me the hospital address and her room number… I'll catch the next flight and will see you soon." Freddie said quickly.

He checked and the last flight that evening had already left. He found one at 6:20 am on Monday. He booked a ticket and asked for a car service to pick him up. He woke up at 4:30 am, put some clothes in his carry-on and left for the La Guardia airport. In Madison he rushed to take a taxi and he was at the hospital at her room before 9:45 in the morning. She was in bed awake with her right arm in a cast. She saw him and started crying. He hugged her from the left side and kissed her warmly on her cheeks. Lisa was there too. When she stopped sobbing she said,

"Why did you come? It's nothing serious I just had a fight defending myself, that's all… I beat him up and you'll be proud of me. I only injured my right arm and my right hip. I'll be okay in few days…" Anne was talking fast, as if from a dream still.

"Take it easy my love, you—you don't have to talk now… I'm glad it's not more serious… and I'm happy to be with you." Freddie motioned her to calm down. She calmed down slowly and he smiled back at her to reassure her that she was safe with him. He could imagine the shock and the fear she had encountered when the guy broke in to her place. But he also knew she was strong enough to get over it soon.

"How was your weekend with the children? Sorry we couldn't talk!" Anne asked.

"It went fine… and they enjoyed staying in the apartment sleeping in proper guest rooms instead on a sofa bed. Matilda dropped them off, and I—I told her about us. She said she's looking forward to meet you. How do you feel now, do you still have a lot of pain?" Freddie asked.

"I don't feel any pain… they keep giving me pain killers and sleeping pills at night. The only pain I have now is my confinement to this bed… Lara came to see me yesterday and spent most of the day sitting on this chair. My parents, especially my Mom, never left me. I didn't want to disturb you, but she found your number on my phone and called you um… when I was asleep. Please don't worry about me. You need to get back soon, I'm sure you have a lot of work to do." Anne said enthused.

"You know you're not a bad talker for a bed-confined person! Can you just relax and feel good that I'm here. I'll leave when I know you're bored with me." Freddie said holding her left hand.

Lisa then interfered and said,

"The doctors said she could go home tomorrow. They'll take an MRI today to check again. She'll be staying with us until they fix her door and a couple of broken furniture. Bjorn is taking care of that as we speak. However, she'll be in no position to—to go to work for at least one week. She also has to use a crutch to support her when she walks. It's her right hip that suffered from some bad bruises when she fell down. She'll explain to you later what happened. When you let her talk."

"Do you have two beds in—in the same room she'll be using at your home?" Freddie asked.

"As a matter of fact we do, it's not her room, but a guest room on the main level. You're welcome to use the other bed if that's what you're asking." Lisa answered.

"I heard that, Yeyyy! You're so sweet to accept that my love! Thank you Mom. Is Dad coming?" Anne asked.

"He should be coming this afternoon... he has a class to teach in half an hour. Why do you ask?" Lisa responded.

"To see if the door is fixed, may be I can go straight to my apartment, I'm not afraid anymore, the monster is behind bars, and my love Fredric is with me." Anne said.

***

Bjorn arrived to the hospital two hours later and was happy to see Freddie there. He said the door is fixed with new locks and the apartment is clean. Anne asked Freddie if it's ok to be there at the apartment for a couple of days until she can start moving around again.

"I'll be happy to be with you the next few days. I can run errands if you allow me to use your car. I will be honored to look after you my dear!"

Freddie and Bjorn sat in the waiting room and chatted together about DAA. Bjorn took notes of what the story is all about and told Freddie he will prepare some remarks and review them with him and Anne. He explained to Freddie the increasing interest in ethical concepts by most bug corporations and government agencies. Bjorn was not surprised that the American Bar Association (ABA) is adamant about the ethical behavior of all its lawyer members. I will review some research I did in this respect sometime ago and will share it with to help you and Anne deliver a strong speech.

Freddie stayed with Anne after having a quick lunch at the hospital cafeteria with Bjorn. Anne was taken for a MRI test after lunch. The doctor told her that the damage to her hand and hip is very mild and she would heal very quickly. Lisa and Bjorn left around 4 pm. Freddie said he will go to a nearby hotel later around 8 pm and will be back in the morning. He sat on a chair next to Anne's bed, holding her hand. They spoke lightly between Anne's short spurs of sleeping. He kissed her when she was awake and that made her feel much better.

Anne wanted to talk about what happened, but Freddie asked her to wait till tomorrow and to rest today. He texted his office to notify them that he may be away for few days and to call him for urgent matters only. Anne was quite sleepy around 8 PM and Freddie excused himself to let her rest. He found and reserved a room at a hotel he found on the online. He called a taxi, wished Anne a restful sleep and told her he'll be back at 8:00 am in the morning.

***

Freddie was back at the hospital at 8:00 the next day and brought Anne some croissant and Danish pastries with fresh coffee. She was happy to see him and hugged him passionately using her free left arm. She told Freddie she slept well and had pleasant dreams about them together in the new apartment in New York. Anne said her pain is slightly reduced and was looking forward to return home the same morning. The nurse asked her to sign release papers and the plan was that she could leave around 10:00 am.

Lisa, Anne's mother showed up at 9:00 am to help her get ready. She said she'll be happy to drive them home, as her first class is not before 11:00 o'clock.

Anne was taken down to the car on a wheelchair accompanied by Lisa and Freddie. She was helped to walk in to her apartment and went straight to bed. Lisa left to go to work and Freddie sat on a chair next to Anne's bed. She felt good enough to report to Freddie what happened, as he was curious to hear the details. She said,

"My ex, Mark found out from friends that I was selling my practice and moving to New York to live with a new 'lover'… He came late on Saturday night banging on the door insisting that I should open the door… I knew it was Mark and he sounded very drunk from the way the spoke. I—I refused to let him in and I called nine-one-one. Before the police arrived six minutes later, he forced his body through the door and broke the locks… As soon as he—he walked in he started swearing and shouting that I had no right to leave him alone in Madison and he grabbed me by my arms and forced me against the wall."

Anne started crying and Freddie asked her to stop talking but she insisted to continue,

"He looked horrible and scary… He continued to blabber and shout and I—I tried my utmost to defend myself by kicking him, as my hands were held tight against the wall… He pushed me to the right, and I fell first on the coffee table and a chair, then on the floor and injured my right arm, and hip. He--He suddenly lost his balance and dropped his body on the sofa. The police arrived and saw us both, me on the floor and Mark wasted and unconscious on the sofa. I—I explained to them briefly what happened and how he forced himself in... They called an ambulance that took me to the hospital and then they woke him up, handcuffed him and took him to the police station."

Anne took a breather and stopped sobbing while firmly holding Freddie's hand. He put his arm around her shoulder and calmed him without saying a word. A minute later he asked Anne if she filed charges against him and she said no. I thought the police record was sufficient to keep him behind bars. Freddie insisted that she should file charges against Mark. He asked her if she has a lawyer to start the process. She nodded and he handed her the phone to call him immediately.

The lawyer came to her place one hour later and heard the story in details and asked if she had more evidence. She told him the police came, took photos of her, Mark and the broken door and furniture. He was satisfied and said he will go straight to the police station, get the evidence and file a complaint. He also said he'll make sure Mark remains behind bars until he appears before a judge in the court.

Two hours later, the lawyer called Anne and told her all is order. Mark is still in custody of the police, and he asked the court clerk to request from the judge an urgent hearing of the case. Both Anne and Freddie felt relieved, and Anne was thankful for Freddie's advice.

It was around 1:00 pm and Freddie ordered lunch to be catered to Anne's apartment. She then rested for an hour after lunch on her queen size bed and Freddie managed to climb next to her on the left side to hug her and help her sleep.

When Anne woke up she was thrilled to find Freddie next to her and hugging her. She said,

"I'm so sorry my love for putting you through all this and I thank you so much for being here next to me... I am determined to heal fast and will soon be with you in New York to launch our project." Anne said confidently.

"No worries my dear! Tell me what does Mark do for a living?" Freddie asked.

"Believe it or not, he is a lawyer too." Anne said

"Oh my goodness, what's with these lawyers and us? Freddie said. Then he took a pause and continued,

"We all go through certain obstacles on the way to a greater future... It is important to cleanse our souls from all evil thoughts and to forgive those who wrongly harm us... Harmful people may cause us some discomfort and short periods of pain, but they are the ones who end up suffering for much longer, and bear the—the consequences of their own awful behavior." Freddie responded.

"Right you are! The key is to learn from our own mistakes also. I made a bad conscious decision when I married Mark. I was focused on his looks and physical charm and thought he was great in and out. I was wrong. . He turned out to be very jealous, violent with his language and sometimes with his hands. I was stupid enough to think he'd change until I realized it was a hopeless case... I dropped him from my life after two years of marriage but his ego did not stop him from continuing to harass me, demanding I was still his." Anne Explained.

"Look at where he is now, in jail and without a job. Let's hope he will learn his own lesson once and for all. Thank goodness he's no more a ghost that would haunt you... He may have caused you some physical discomfort, but never will he will never weaken your strong character and determination to move on with your life. I—I love this inner feature that you possess, along with your extraordinary external beauty."

"Sweetheart, keep talking... your sweet words heal me faster and I adore you!" Anne said with a big smile gracing her face.

"Tell me, do you feel pain from your hip when you walk, even with the crutches?" Freddie asked.

"Some, still! But take a look at the blue purple marks on the side of my hip. That will take a while to dissipate... The cast on my arm should be removed soon as they did not find a serious fracture. So all is well... I will be me, the person you're used to know, very soon!" Anne remarked.

"Good! Before I forget, I had a good conversation with your father about the speech to the forthcoming ABA conference... He took some notes and said he will relay to us some thoughts and ideas to incorporate in the speech... Seemingly he is very well versed on the subject on unethical legal behavior as well."

"My father is a brilliant man and a great professor… All his students love him. He has a way of interpreting concepts that are unique in academic circles. I'm happy to see him involved in our own endeavors. He's also warming up to you, which I love… My mother is already crazy about you. They both don't easily show their affectionate feelings, but I know them well… I used to be like that, however America changed within me the cold characteristics of the Swedish culture that I was born into." Anne said.

"There is nothing cold about you, my love! Your lips are so hot they fire me up; your body is so gorgeous it regularly generates heat; and above all, your smile, and your—your soul are so splendid, they melt any glacier in the Himalayas." Freddie narrated passionately. And leaned over to kiss her. Anne started sobbing and responded,

"Keep talking! I am so blessed by your poetic words and sincere expressions. It is you—you and your electric vibrations that ignite all the fire and warmth you're describing about me. I—I am so grateful to God for this blessing and I will do my best to maintain this fire glowing between us." Anne said passionately.

Soon after 6:00 pm, Lisa and Bjorn, Lara and John, all came to see Anne and brought with them bouquets of lowers and boxes of chocolate. They were glad to see me around and brought chairs from the dining area and sat around Anne. They talked about their daily jobs and managed to crack few jokes to cheer her up. Lara assured Anne not to worry about her patients, as she took a week off from her work and decided to handle all Anne's appointments while she is recovering. Lara added,

"They seem to like me too… so that encourages me to proceed with enthusiasm for the task ahead."

"That's good news… something good comes out of this unexpected ugly episode. I'm glad you are easing into the future work, Lara." Anne said gleefully.

John and Lara left an hour later, and Bjorn handed Freddie a printed three-page document and said,

"This is for you and Anne to consider… I put some thoughts down on paper, and I'm available to elaborate, in case your need further clarifications."

"Wow! Thank you so much… you are certainly efficient, and this is a great incentive for us to eventually deliver a forceful speech. Anne and I will look into it later in the evening. Thanks!" Freddie said.

"Dad, we really appreciate your help and guidance in this regard. Thank you, and I love you!" Anne stated.

Freddie then suggested that he could order dinner from a restaurant to deliver and they can all enjoy a meal together with Anne. They all agreed on what to eat and the food arrived 30 minutes later. Anne insisted they all sit around the round dining table, and Freddie helped her to be seated and added cushions to soften the position of her hip, and was delighted to see her use her left hand to hold the fork.

The parents left after dinner and Freddie asked Anne to read the notes from her father loud. That took a good 15 minutes, during which they both said 'wow' after every written idea. Anne showed him how to make a copy from the small machine she had at home.

They slept well that night and Anne persuaded Freddie to fly back the next day.

CHAPTER 15

A Brighter Moonlight

The cast was removed from Anne's hand, and was able to walk normally after twelve days from Freddie's return to New York. They kept in touch on a daily basis, and apprised one another about the ongoing progress on either side.

Freddie briefed Anne that the office space should be ready in about one week. He added that the Judge agreed to reduce Jane's sentence to 8 months, and the publicists will submit their plan, with the logo for the branding of DAA, in 5 days. Melody will start working at DAA the following week, and the website is almost ready.

Anne told him that she managed to go to the office ten days after his return, and was very pleased with Lara's professional work with the clients during her absence. The official transfer of practice will take place within 4 days; and the response to the letters sent out to Anne's clients was quite positive.

Additionally, Anne said that the judge heard Mark's case and saw the evidence of his violent action. He sentenced him to serve three years in Jail, and pay Anne an amount of $250,000 within 30 days. The judge also disbarred Mark from practicing law in the state of Minnesota. Anne decided to implement her move to New York within one week. The apartment will be sublet furnished as is, to friends of her family.

As regards the speech, and apart from the notes they exchanged by email, Anne and Freddie agreed to work on it when they are together within short.

***

Freddie flew to Madison one day before Anne's scheduled journey to New York. He helped Anne with her four suitcases of personal belongings. He booked first class seats to ensure her comfort. Laura had arranged a spacious van to pick them up for their journey home from La Guardia airport. The flight landed on time and they arrived home at 6:30 pm. When he opened the door, Freddie and Anne were surprised to see Barry, Melody and Laura inside, who yelled 'welcome home'. There were banners hanging from the ceiling with similar wording.

They hugged one another, and Barry popped the champagne. They sat together in the living room cheering the new 'arrivals'. They appreciated the sight of several bouquets of flowers, a tray of yummy canapés and a box of Belgian chocolate. Laura had arranged this welcome without the knowledge of her boss. Anne was touched by this unexpected surprise and was elated to be at her new home in the Big Apple. They all talked cheerfully for 40 minutes, then Freddie invited them out to dinner, to celebrate Anne's addition to the 'family'.

The doorman brought the luggage to their apartment and Anne decided to open it later. Then they all went down to enjoy dinner together. No one talked about what Anne had gone through, or anything that had to do with the past. They were mindful and focused, on the future life ahead.

When they returned from Dinner, Anne was so excited about the new home and took time to walk with Freddie on the balcony, admiring the night skyline of Manhattan and the Queens borough in the distance. She then opened one suitcase and took out her toiletries and bathrobes. Freddie ran the bathtub with hot water for her to take a bath and relax. He noticed that her hip bruises were practically fading. He went down on his knees and kissed the marked area. That tickled Anne and made her giggle. Then she asked him to join her in the big tub and he did not hesitate. They played and splashed with laughs of happiness and joy.

Then they slept very comfortably in the king size bed with their bodies closely attached to one another.

***

They took it easy the next day despite their schedule for several meetings with various people during the day. The architect met them at the office space and showed them around. The first two floors were finished beautifully and some work was being completed on the upper floors. The chosen furniture for lower floors was in place and looked very welcoming and professionally placed. Anne's office upstairs was expanded and getting painted. The architect asked her to choose between various furniture options for her own space. She naturally chose a simple modern design with comfortable sofa for guests and an impressive therapist chair across.

They later went to Freddie's office and faced a similar welcome from the staff. They cheerfully stood up to greet them. Anne waved back with a big smile. As usual she looked dazzling in her casual jeans, her top and her flat shoes. Laura had arranged for a meeting with the publicist in the conference room to update them on their work. She showed them different designs for the logo and signage. She advised them of the various events to be held, including TV media promotion, journal and radio advertising, a VIP list of 100 dignitaries to be invited for the office inauguration… and so on.

Laura had also arranged for two secretarial candidates she chose to be interviewed by Anne an hour later. Both were experienced and presentable secretaries. The one that would be hired would eventually report to Melody, the executive secretary. Freddie asked Laura to have their own receptionist/office manager to work for the organization, as she's very good, and to find a replacement to work in the company.

The job agency was searching for an experienced manager position in the field of marketing and fund raising. Two candidates were scheduled for an interview with Freddie and Anne, the next day. Freddie said he will have on of his many accountants to move to DAA to help set the programs for an eventual accountant to be hired.

So, basically the initial organization team was being put in place at an efficient pace and the official office inauguration was planned to take place on a Monday at 5 pm, 20 days later.

***

While waiting for the work on the office space, the website, hiring the initial staff, and preparing for the inauguration, Anne and Freddie spent some time drafting their speeches to give at the conference due in a couple of weeks. Laura had informed the ABA organizers that both the chairman and the CEO of DAA will present their words in two consecutive parts to the conferees.

The first part by Freddie would be to share what happened and how disappointed everyone was to learn about the misconduct by the lawyers and the sentence they received from the court.

Anne's part was to introduce the new organization DAA and explain its mission and its strategy to succeed and expand its outreach to other major cities in the nation.

They both shared their drafts with James and Bjorn for their final editing and modifications where required.

Meanwhile the work in the office space was completed and the work was commenced 10 days before the inauguration. Melody was on board, as executive assistant reporting to Anne and Freddy. Anne hired an experienced woman in her early forties, as vice president responsible for marketing and outreach. Her name was Vera Hartford, previously employed as senior vice president of a large non-profit organization. The accountant, a secretary and a receptionist were in place as well.

The space itself was quite impressive and decorated with very good taste, and furnished with high quality desks, chairs and other fixtures. The lighting was designed to enhance the look of the space that also featured various plants and flowers that gave a very relaxed yet professional atmosphere. In addition to the wide reception area, there were four executive offices and a spacious conference room on the first two levels, connected by a spiraling staircase.

An adjacent garden of about 700 square feet outside the first level was beautifully planted around its borders with flowers and small trees around the main stone-floored area. A huge glass window divided the garden from the first level and added more natural light and beauty to the space itself.

Freddie and Anne gathered everyone the first day of work in the reception area to welcome them to DAA. Freddie as the founder and chairman introduced Anne, the CEO of the organization. He then asked her to explain the mission to the new staff. When Anne finished her talk, Freddie asked them to go to the conference room to have some champagne to wish DAA a successful future. The initial staff enjoyed the company of their top management and an hour was spent getting to know one another.

***

On the day of the Grand Opening, Anne and Freddie reviewed the impressive list of guests invited. It included top executives of big corporations and major banks, the Mayor of New York city and other key government officials, heads of charity organizations, board members of the American Bar Association, and key friends and family, including Anne's Parents and Freddie's mother.

The weather was good and a soft early fall breeze helped to enhance the comfort of the occasion.

Top caterers served cocktails and canapés and spread several small round tables in the reception area and the outside garden. Elegantly printed pocketsize brochures about DAA were placed on several corners and desks inside, for the guests to take. Soft classical music played in the background. The publicist stood next to Freddie and Anne near the entrance to introduce them to the guests. The hosts looked gorgeous, Freddie in a formal tuxedo, and Anne in a dazzling evening Gown. A signing book for the guests to write their names was placed on a table next to a large silver plate for guests to drop their business cards as well.

A TV crew and other selected journalists were roaming around recording and asking questions or comments from the invited VIP guests.

Once most of the guests entered inside, Freddie motioned for their attention to welcome them. He gave a short speech explaining what inspired him to establish the non-profit Organization; followed by Anne who shared her ideas and plans for the future of DAA. She also told the guests she's counting on their donations and support. They were both applauded and cheered, while some guests whispered in the ears of their companions how awesome the hosts looked together.

The gathering lasted about 90 minutes. The publicist said 97 guests had showed up. Melody and the other secretaries collected the business cards and agreed to sort them out the next day. They also noticed that about 75 brochures were taken. Freddie and Anne were very satisfied with the event and hoped it will be the beginning of greater success to follow.

Freddie's invited his mother, and Anne's parents to dinner, along with Barry and Melody. Mary was reluctant in the beginning, but Anne convinced her to stay for a short while, and her driver will take care back home comfortably. She liked Anne and was happy to meet her parents, so she agreed to stay a bit longer. Mary had always liked Barry and she congratulated him and Melody on their forthcoming wedding.

The evening went well with a lot of talk about some of the guests that came, many of whom, Mary had known already. Anne emphasized the task to follow through and ask the guests to donate. Anne was completely healed and she was comfortable standing throughout the joyful event.

Anne spent the evening mostly paying attention to Mary who left early to go home. Bjorn and Lisa were also pleased to meet Barry and Melody. They spent another hour together before they ended a lovely evening. Anne walked next to her mother while Freddie walked with Bjorn, in their short walk back home.

Her parents were highly grateful to Freddie's hospitality and the planned attractions they visited during the weekend. They truly loved the new apartment and appreciated the comfortable guestroom where they stayed. They were mostly delighted to see their daughter so happy with her new job, also enjoying a great relationship with Freddie. The plan was to discuss with Bjorn the final drafts for the speeches the next morning, and before they fly back to Madison in the afternoon.

***

Bjorn was satisfied with the drafts of the two speeches by Freddie and Anne. They had lunch on the balcony at the apartment, prepared by Anne and her mother who gave the credit to her daughter for the delicious pasta with Alfredo truffle sauce. Freddie was impressed that Anne cooked and joked about it. She told him,

"That's it, no more food for you!"

"I'm impressed! You said you only know how to fry eggs. That's good to know that we will not starve around here. Anyhow, congratulations. Come here and let me hug you!" Freddie responded.

The parents were so happy to see their daughter cracking jokes with Freddie. They were glad they came, thanked them for a wonderful visit and wished them a very happy and successful future together. The car arranged by Freddie was waiting for them downstairs to take them to the airport.

Around 2:30 pm, Freddie and Anne walked back to the DAA office for an update on the outcome of the opening event the day before. Melody showed them articles by two journals and one magazine with scenes of the event and a photo of Freddie and Anne. The contents were positive applauding the humanitarian actions taken by the founder Fredric Rodman, and his new girl friend Dr. Anne Stevenson, the CEO of the organization. The receptionist Amanda told them that she received 9 phone calls already from other media companies asking for interviews.

The TV channel that covered the event said they will feature the event at the seven pm Evening News. Freddie was already known in the news media from his prior interviews, and this time the focus was on Anne, who was also referred to in one article as the "New Humanitarian Queen". The article underlined her beauty and her high education, and wrote that, "She was bound to attract the attention of many women to the fold".

"You are a celebrity now my dear!" Freddie said when her read the article.

"Fine, this will not shift my focus from the work to be done. Fame… mame… all that is secondary." Anne said humbly.

"What matters now is to build on the momentum we started and publicize our work in specific women organization and figure out areas of cooperation." Freddie said.

"I will work closely with Melody to do research online, and get a list of all the names of women-related organizations in the tri-state-area of New York, New Jersey and Connecticut… We will contact them and ask for introductory meetings and discussions. This way they will learn about our motives and strengths, and hope to attract the attention of their members to participate in our mission." Anne explained.

"Also, as regards the new requested interviews, I suggest we accept them all and the more we spread the word the more people will learn about us and our mission." Freddie added.

"I couldn't agree more my love… If you like I can handle all these interviews myself. You focus on your work and trust me that I'll do a good job." Anne suggested.

"Not only a good job… no one can do a better job than you." Freddie said emphatically.

***

Anne spent the rest of the week handling these interviews in the conference room of DAA offices. The reports about her and the organization were very favorably written. Her beautiful photo appeared in most of the articles and that encouraged other media companies to ask for more of her time.

Meanwhile, Melody and Vera contacted all the women organizations they found online, and arranged for meetings in the days that followed. By the beginning of the following week, DAA received 4 calls from separate women who asked if they could personally meet with Dr. Anne Stevenson. Amanda asked what the meeting will be about and they all said, "it is confidential and we prefer to discuss with Dr. Stevenson". Anne told Melody to fix appointments with all four women. She said she will see them in her private office on the fourth floor in the next two days.

The women that had called arrived at separate times as per the schedule given to them by Melody, who escorted them to meet with the 'boss' upstairs. After every sessions, one could see tears freshly dried up by a couple of them. They all carried a big smile on their faces, however. They were mesmerized by Anne's compassion and good advice for the different stories they shared with Anne.

They were in their late twenties/early thirties, and the four admitted that they were taken advantage and humiliated by married men. The common element was the fact they were obliged to perform weird sexual favors in return for the money they regularly received. They all said they were selling their dignity along with their bodies. Two of the women had good jobs, which they abandoned for the sake of making more money.

Anne told them she can help them regain their dignity if they were seriously willing to change. She explained that the only choice was to pursue an honorable way of life, learn a skill if they don't have one, and be less greedy about money. She reminded them that DAA was established with the mission to help women with similar cases free of charge.

The other two women expressed their misery that they felt enslaved by the married men they were seeing. Anne made them aware that fear can be overcome when substituted with self-love and inner desire to change. They asked if they could become her private patients. Anne advised them to plan similar visits twice a week for a while, and it is OK if they can't afford to pay her fees as a therapist. The women said they have money to pay.

Anne told all of them that DAA plans to have classes in the near future to teach women new skills if required. She told each one of them before they left to coordinate their visits with Melody who is very trustworthy. Anne also encouraged them to refer DAA to other friends they know that are in similar situations. Melody took their personal information on their way out and hugged each one of them before they left.

Anne was thrilled by the visits of these four women and it was a good sign about the validity of the project and its future. Freddie was enthused to see her feeling good about this start in such a short period of time, and assured Anne to expect continued progress at a higher level. She reminded him that if the number of people seeking help increases dramatically, DAA may need additional classrooms. Freddie told her that was a minor issue as he can easily find other spaces available to satisfy her needs.

Few more days were left before the commencement of ABA conference, and they rehearsed with one another the prepared speeches to be given.

***

The day arrived for Freddie and Anne to appear before the large number of delegates who came to New York City, to attend the annual ABA conference. Their speeches were scheduled at 10:30 in the morning of the second day. Fredric Rodman was properly introduced as a big real estate businessman and the abused victim of a unethical act. He will tell you about it himself. Fredric rose from his chair where he was seated next to Anne behind the stage podium and he heard a loud applause in advance of his speech. Then he said,

> *"Thank you!... Thank you...*
> *I am honored to be here and share with you the reason why I was asked to speak to you this morning.*
> *We all attempt to do our best as good citizens for the benefit of mankind. You are all professionals and you work hard to uphold your self-esteem and legitimate moral practice, according to the code of conduct, set by the American Bar Association, of which you are members.*
> *I am not a lawyer myself. I am your average working businessman who was also saddled with shortsighted*

imperfections as a human being. I made many mistakes in my life, as many of us do, but in my case I paid a high price. One major mistake, which cost me the breakup of my family unit, had a huge lesson waiting for me too. I learned that immoral or unethical behavior cannot be escaped without punishment and unbearable suffering. What goes around comes around, as we know. It took me a long while to rise up again, and to learn how to embrace life with a new mindset of decency, and a genuine desire to put other people's interest ahead of mine.

Many of you have already heard my story from journals you may have read or TV shows you may have seen. Briefly, and for the sake of those who haven't, I dated a woman after I deserted my family to pursue physical pleasures. Though it took me a while to learn how wrong and meaningless that was, I finally developed the courage to break up with the woman I was seeing. Shortly after the break up I was kidnapped, beaten, and then thrown in front of a hospital entrance to treat severe fractures of my chest ribs. All because I did not pay a ransom of $2 million to the woman who allegedly was the one behind all this.

To cut the story short, it was later revealed during court hearings that the mastermind behind the whole affair was a practicing lawyer. His own client, the same woman confessed to the court that it was him who sponsored and coerced her to be the front villain for the dirty job. It was also revealed that his other two partners were running similar operations, mainly sponsoring and coercing young beautiful women to hunt rich married men. The women were used to suck as much money as they can from their men.

Other cases, besides mine, were also found. They hired hit men to harass and threaten the men who wanted out from their relationships with the women. In most cases they obliged the men to ultimately pay handsome amounts of money, if they wanted their affairs to remain secret. When the judge learned that the other partners were also guilty, he instructed the FBI to raid the the law firm offices and to confiscate all their files. With the evidence found, he ordered the arrest of the other two partners and disbarred all three of them. They are now serving 8 t0 10 years in jail. The law firm doors were ordered closed for good, and punitive monetary damages were additionally imposed. The woman I dated was sentenced to serve a 3-year term.

I agreed to appear in front of you today for two reasons. One is to encourage every one of you to abide by the code of conduct that your esteemed association has written, and second is to share with you how I was inspired to turn this ugly incident into an opportunity to serve others.

You certainly know ABA's code of conduct much better that me. I read some of the rules that you follow and I was highly impressed by the high standards of the legal ethics and the professional responsibility expected of every member. You don't need me to tell you how to perform your professional duties, or how to obey the law, and how to put your clients interests ahead of yours.

You have such an honorable profession, and despite the false accusations by a few who criticize your work as a means to claim status and wealth instead of helping others, your contribution to the justice system continues to be priceless. The bias toward professionals like is old. Perhaps you are aware of the joke, when Shakespeare's quotation in one of his plays, read "First, let's kill all the lawyers." This prejudiced opinion may have continued among many, but is rare. It definitely contradicts the moral ground that legitimizes your remarkable task.

As you move forward, try to remember what Associate Justice Benjamin Cardozo one said, "Law never is, but is always about to be." And "we are what we believe we are." As a non-professional myself, I continue to have faith in your profession and its future, and I commend you for the very important job you are doing to serve humanity.

Now, allow me to share with you the inspiration I had as a result of this inflicted experience. I decided to create a non-profit organization I call, "Dignity Above All" or DAA, the details of which I leave to my much better looking and capable partner who is with us here. I present to you the CEO of DAA, Dr. Anne Stevenson."

Freddie sat down and turned the podium over to Anne. As soon as she stood up, looking dazzling with her elegant dark pantsuit and accentuated by a white silk scarf around her neck, every one in the hall cheered and clapped. They admired her astonishing beauty and aura, as also shown on the big screens for everyone to see. When the big room quieted down, Anne spoke,

Good morning ladies and gentlemen... Isn't Mr. Rodman a great guy? (She paused, and a new wave of applaud started again) I am privileged to be his partner in life and his trust in me to lead this new non-profit organization that he founded. When I finally understood the mission of DAA, after listening to his story on TV, and learning about the suffering he went through, I decided to accept his offer to run this organization, and I turned over my private practice as a psychoanalyst in Madison, Wisconsin to join him. (Anne was interrupted for a few seconds when apparently some fellow citizens of Wisconsin stood up shouting words of good cheer.) Anne smiled graciously and then continued, I am convinced that our mission at DAA is not only noble but also very feasible. I don't know how many of you saw Fredric's interview on PBS a while ago, it is worth repeating what he said about his goals for DAA, I quote:

1. *To bring awareness to young women to avoid, be it on their own, or if coerced by others, any seductive or harassing acts with well-to-do men whom they find vulnerable to fall in their traps.*

2. To provide these women who agree to join DAA, the proper guidance and education to seek other alternatives, with greater dignity and self-esteem.
3. To help find respectable jobs for these women with their own skills or with new skills from the education programs they will receive from DAA.
4. To ask the ones that DAA helps out, to pledge continued assistance by attracting other women they know, not to be tempted to go their old way, and to recruit others to spread the word about the organization.
5. To create a monthly free publication that will reach all national subscribers to DAA, with professional opinions and articles, alerting its readers how to avoid potential damages that could occur as a result of their negligence.
6. To bring awareness to men also, about the values of loyalty, by not pursuing relationships outside their marriage as they could end up destroying their family units by going through ugly divorces.
7. To create other DAA centers in major cities around the nation, and to raise funds to cover additional expansion costs."

My job is to simply execute the above goals with workable strategies and approaches. We started our operation a week ago. Mr. Rodman did not tell you that he doubled the initial working capital of the organization from his own money, and gave us a big elegant space for our beautiful headquarters rent-free.

We had the honor to receive about 100 VIP guests from the region, including members of ABA board of directors, who came to our grand opening. Many have blessed our presence and pledged their support to our organization. We are also constructing a dynamite website to publicize our work and expand our outreach across the nation. That is in addition to our monthly magazine featuring main events and articles.

We will have a professional staff of not less than twenty people to implement our campaign.

I am also encouraged by the fact that in the short period since we started, I already received a handful of beautiful women, unsolicited, came to seek a definite change from their current immoral relationships with married men. They asked me to help them live a new life with honor and dignity. I know we will succeed, and I also know we can do a more effective job with your support and generous gifts.

We welcome any of you to come and visit us to see what we do, and to meet our staff. By the way, we have very good Italian espresso machine, so come! Thank you, and God Bless this great country of ours!

Every one stood up and applauded Anne for her encouraging words and good sense of humor. It was evident how much she was admired. Freddie got off his chair and they both stood in the middle of the stage holding their hands up together, as a gesture of appreciation.

Freddie and Anne felt wonderful afterwards and they walked out with their heads high, accompanied by the organizer of the event, who promised to send them a copy of the video tape recording. Anne immediately thought she will upload that on the new website.

That video triggered a huge interest on the part of many viewers and donations started coming in form many different directions.

CHAPTER 16

The Sun Takes Over From the Moon

A lot was accomplished during the first two months of DAA. The website received hundreds of visitors every day and the monthly magazine reached a circulation of close to1000 subscribers. Thirty donors registered their names on the site and pledged a total of $375,000 a year. Big banks and corporations sent one time checks totaling $1.6 million. Vera the vice president did an excellent job contacting most of the VIP's that came to the Grand Opening event.

Anne hired more people and DAA had a total of 12 employees. Anne had18 private clients that confided in her as a therapist, albeit only half of them were treated pro bono. More interviews were lined up including some from out of state including an interview with a major newspaper from California.

Four classrooms on the third floor were used to teach women new skills. Teachers were all volunteers who signed up to help DAA. Three courses were taught, secretarial work and typing, housing keeping and Childcare, and basic accounting or bookkeeping.

The door was always open during the day for visitors to walk in and inquire further about the messages posted on a board outside, just below the large DAA sign. Freddie insisted on hiring a security guard that stood by the main entrance to ensure the caliber of the visitors and the safety of the employees.

The working conditions were excellent and the employees were all happy being part of the organization. They had tremendous respect for Anne and her humane style of management and her incredible creative ideas. Freddie came to DAA almost daily for a couple of hours and had his own office next to Anne's on the first level. They often met together to discuss what was going on and how they can grow further.

***

On a personal level, Freddie was super delighted to see the relationship that Anne had developed with his two boys. He often heard them laugh together and go shipping with Anne alone. She treated them with utmost respect and always reminded them of the importance of their parents love for them. Matilda came to visit once and met Anne and found her to be as wonderful as the kids had mentioned from their prior visits. Once a month Freddie, Anne and the two boys drove to Greenwich to visit Mary who loved to have them and spoil them with gifts and good food.

The wedding of Barry and Melody was to take place within two weeks. Anne and Melody became close friends during and outside the office. They frequently visited one another, and Melody privately showed Anne how to cook meatloaf, Freddie's favorite. Even the children loved the meatloaf that Anne once prepared, and that surprised Freddie, who appreciated her cooking it.

I became even closer to Freddie the past few months. Our friendship was certainly becoming a brotherly relationship. One evening he asked Melody and me to go down with him and Anne to the 20th floor in the same building. I could understand why he was doing this. He had the keys to an apartment and he opened the door. The place was vacant and I asked him,

"What are you doing Freddie, why are we here?"

"Just look around and tell me if you like it." Freddie said.

I walked around to see the apartment with Melody. I kept asking her why the heck is he showing us this place, is he planning to use it as new offices for Anne's private practice? There were two spacious bedrooms with their own bathrooms, a large living/dining area and an open big kitchen. A fairly good-sized balcony with a nice view East toward Queens. After two minutes we finished with tour and I asked Freddie again,

"So is this some kind of a test you are putting us through? What game are you playing now?"

"Did you like it?" Freddie asked.

"Of course we did it is a fabulous place." I responded

"Good, it is yours, our wedding gift to you and Melody!" Freddie answered.

"Freddie, please don't say that. I have a weak heart, stop joking." I said. I looked at him and expected him to laugh. Instead,

"I am serious… it's yours. You're my brother and that is the least I can do to thank you for putting up with me all these years. The family owns it and you are part of the family, you have always been!"

At that moment I knew he was serious. Melody and I looked at one another and with misty eyes we both walked toward him and gave him a big hug. Anne was so touched by the scene and she ran to joining them for a bigger hug still. That was one of the longest hugs I've seen and it is very sentimental. I then looked at Freddie alone and gave him a big kiss on his cheek and I said, "Thank you…thank you and again thank you."

Freddie gave me the keys to the apartment and said,

"You can move in anytime you want, you'll get the deed within a week." Freddie said.

"Yey, I'm so excited we are going be neighbors soon. You two are brothers, Melody and I are sisters." Anne said passionately.

"Good, now let's go up and pop the champagne." Freddie said.

***

It took me a couple of days to digest Freddie's gift and I never knew that friendship can flourish to the extent. Melody and I were eternally grateful for his generosity and we agreed to wait till after the wedding and furnish with all new furniture to be discussed with an interior designer. I said I'll give the landlord a 60-day notice to vacate the rented apartment, and that should give us plenty of time to make it ready to move into.

I couldn't get over the new person Freddie has become, particularly since he started admiring Anne several months ago and right after his ugly situation with Jane and the lawyers. He's become well known and highly respected in the city and DAA cemented his fame with Anne even further.

We were ready for the wedding this coming Saturday afternoon at the Lighthouse on Pier 60 facing the Hudson River. We invited about 200 relatives and friends from both sides. Though I am not a religious person Melody insisted to have a Rabbi officiating the wedding. The planner took care of all the arrangements for the reception and the seated dinner that followed in the big hall. We chose to have one best man and one maid of honor. Freddie, my closest friend was my choice. Melody asked Anne, who gracefully agreed to be the maid of honor.

The wedding commenced at 5:00 pm on the last Saturday in October. The view to the water and the sunset that followed, created an enchanting scene that set the pace for a beautiful celebration. Melody walked in with her father who delivered her to me waiting under the canopy. She circled around me 7 times in keeping with the tradition, representing the 7 days of creation. After several minutes of rituals, we exchanged our vows, and the rabbi announced us as husband and wife. That signaled me to kiss Melody, and break the glass under my foot.

Freddie and Anne looked gorgeous, smiling happily all the time. I was relieved when the rituals were over. Melody excused herself to change her wedding dress and put on something lighter. Cocktails and canapés were served to the guests outside the dining room. When they were all seated inside at the designated tables, around he dance floor, Mr. and Mrs. Barry Green were announced entering the room, and every one cheered and clapped. The first dance by the bride and the bridegroom initiated the party and the dance floor was opened for others to follow.

I could not resist the tradition of being carried by women sitting on a chair neither did Melody refuse men to carry her on another chair too. The dance music was invigorating and the dance floor was crowded with guests having fun. Shortly thereafter and while dinner was being served, Freddie clicked on his glass with a knife to attract the attention of people sitting around their dinner tables. When the room quieted down, he stood up and said,

> *"As the best man I wanted to say a word about the bridegroom, my dear friend and brother… He and I go back more than 20 years. We were college and university buddies and continued to keep a close friendship ever since. Barry had always been my mentor and sounding board. He always tried to control my pursuit of stupid ideas, and when I did not listen to him, he continued to keep his open arms and his door unlocked,*

welcoming me to lean on his shoulder, at any hour of the day. That is a good friend for all of us to emulate.
Let us all raise our glasses and drink to him and to his lovely wife Melody, and wish them both a very happy future, which they richly deserve."

I immediately stood up not only to thank him but to say a few words too. I said,

"I first want to thank you all for celebrating this special event with us this evening. I thank my parents for their love and sacrifice to ensure my continued education and my good mannerism. I thank my sweet Melody, my wife, for her true love and acceptance of me as her husband. I promise to always be there for her, and to reciprocate the abundant love and joy of life she showers me with.
"I like to respond to Freddie's words about me, and I want you all to know that his friendship was never an imposition on me. I chose to be his friend because he is unique. He has a loving heart, and an amazing mind. His humanitarian deeds, and his tremendous generosity cannot be matched anywhere else. His transformation through the years to be the great man he is today is a great lesson for me. His friendship provides me great joy that any friend would hope for. And to see beautiful and intelligent Anne by his side is a true reward from heaven. Melody and I love them dearly. Again thank you all, and please have a good time for the rest of the night."

The two couples hugged and kissed while the guests applauded them and congratulated their unique friendship. I told Freddie that we're going to Hawaii for a week's honeymoon.

***

Freddie and Anne went home around midnight feeling happy to have participated in the marriage of their best friends.

Before going to bed they sat for a while and Anne asked Freddie,

"How do you feel now that your best male friend is married?"

"I'm very happy for him… He chose a nice lady and he deserves to settle down now. How about you, um …do you feel happy for them too?" Freddie responded.

"Of course, the marriage of two love birds is very touching and beautiful… Do you--you itch to get married again, and has the occasion sparked any interest on your part?" Anne sweetly asked.

"Sweetheart, um…you know where I stand in this regard… It is your call not mine."

"That's true, I remember telling you that several months ago. That was me then and it's a different me now! Honestly, and after I got to know more closely, I am getting over my fast fears that were caused by my the horrible behavior of my ex. I am much more open to the idea now." Anne said pensively.

"Wow! That's a revealing change of mindset. I'm so glad to hear you say that! So, there is a chance that you may not turn me down if I were to propose to you?" Freddie asked facetiously.

"What? Is it too late in the night for you to understand what I just said?" Anne replied, with a smile.

"May I sleep on it?" Freddie said, and he drew her closely for a big hug and with a smile on his face.

"Take your time my dearest prince charming! You put up with me and waited for a quite a while, waiting for my 'changed mindset'. I—I guess it is my turn now to wait for you. Who knows, you could be scared of the concept of 'forever together' all of a sudden?" Anne said teasingly.

"My love, I am thrilled to know that you—you are amenable to consider me as a potential candidate to be your future husband… And I will now develop enough inner confidence, to trust the fact that I may not be rejected by the woman whom I deeply and truly love." Freddie said passionately.

"How sweet! Again I say, take your time… May be you need to do some more soul searching within? Remember I'm still very young, but you are getting older." Anne said jokingly.

"I love you my pumpkin! Can we go to sleep now?" Freddie said.

"Not until you kiss and hug me passionately, and make love to me like you've never done before." Anne insisted.

"That will be a great honor, my love!"

***

The happy couple took it easy, and got out of bed late on Sunday morning. They had a very restful sleep after an enjoyable Saturday, which was highlighted by the wedding of their best friends and followed by the enlightening conversation thereafter.

"So, Did you sleep on it?" Anne asked with a coffee cup in her hand.

"I slept well thanks, but I forget about what I should sleep on?" Freddie said sarcastically.

"You're trying to be cute again, right?" Anne responded.

"Sweetheart, I'm so impressed by your revised interest in the subject we talked about, and your eagerness anticipating my prompt action in this regard. Can you remind me again what you were expecting me to say or do? You said, I'm getting old and my memory could have become rusty?" Freddie said in a joking mood.

"OK forget it, you don't love me anymore!" Anne teased.

"Oh poor baby! Come sit in my lap. You can cry on my shoulder. I will show you how much I love you!" Freddie responded with a fake sad look on his face.

"I'm so glad you are amused by my mysterious wishful desire. Fine! I'll give you three more days to—to think about it; and if I don't hear from you by then, I—I will pack my bags and go back to Madison." Anne said pretending to be angry, while lifting her eyebrows. They discovered a teasing method in their talks.

"It's a deal! I love ultimatums." Freddie said to conclude the semi-serious discussion. Then they instantly shifted their conversation to what to do the rest of the day. Anne suggested a long walk in Central Park and a lunch at their favorite Italian restaurant.

While walking, Anne told Freddie that Lara is doing well with her practice and who calls her every couple of days with an update. She told him how Lara always thanks them for directing her to take on the work. The Freddie asked Anne,

"Now that several weeks have passed, how do you evaluate our work together at DAA?"

"It is much better that what I even imagined, my love! I am so glad I—I decided to come and be with you, and to share your life endeavors. It's a dream come true for me… I'm living with the best man any woman would love to be with, plus I am doing a benevolent job that thrills me to no end. I—I also love being in New York, and its buzz… The City has amazing cultural events and attractions and we—we both live in one of the most beautiful homes, up in the sky." Anne explained.

"I'm so happy to hear you say that. I also want to—to thank you for the compassionate love you share with my two boys… They adore you, and their mother is now challenged to—to treat them the way you do. What you're doing is priceless to me. I hope one day you will be amenable to change your mind and agree to have a child with me…Oops! Did I say something too soon? OK it's your turn now, I'll run for cover…" Freddie said while covering his face with his hands.

"Mamma Mia, here we go again! He wants to have a child with me before he proposes to marry me? Now, how am I to—to understand that? I will walk inside the church next door and… ask Virgin Mary for an answer." Anne responded surprisingly! Freddie couldn't stop laughing and the only thing he could was to hug her and say,

"I am so happy to notice these happy changes in your character and I—I really enjoy your morbid sense of humor. OK I get the message… we'll go step by step. Agree?"

"Fine, just speed up your steps please!" Anne muttered quietly.

"I promise you I will… and I love you!" Freddie ended the conversation on a good note.

***

Monday was a busy day at DAA. Anne had four private sessions scheduled with women seeking guidance on how to break up wrongful relationships with married men. Three more sessions with women were scheduled for the following day.

Vera and Melody were busy answering dozens of requests from other women asking for classes to develop certain work skills. Others offered to do volunteer work at DAA if needed.

DAA received a $150,000 check, donation from the American Bar Association, with a thank you letter from the board of directors for the speech given during the conference. The letter also stated that the board sent out letters to their members encouraging them to donate as well. Donation request cards were inserted in the monthly magazines they sent out and about 100 responses with an average of $70 a month were received from various individuals already.

Freddie had to attend to several meetings to decide whether to invest in new properties his team had worked on in advance. He also reminded his manager to work on the deed to give to Barry upon his return from his honeymoon. Anne was extremely grateful for adding her as an equal owner of the apartment. Besides, she requested that he stops paying her salary as CEO of DAA shortly after the opening but Freddie refused to listen she felt very secure and she did not need extra money.

On Tuesday evening Freddie told her that he heard about a very good restaurant in the city called Daniel, named after the name of the chef owner and who earned a 2-michelin star rating. He told Anne that he reserved a table on Friday at 8:00 pm, and they both should dress elegantly to enjoy this romantic evening at this posh place.

Anne was excited to have this evening with her Fredric, and she had a gorgeous Ferrari-red dress on with a beautiful pair of low-heel red shoes. She also selected a nice dark blue suit for Fredric to wear with a white shirt and sharp-looking red tie.

They were warmly received at the fancy restaurant and seated at a quiet corner table in the elegantly decorated dining room. Freddie ordered an exquisite bottle of champagne, and the headwaiter showed them the five-course menu prepared by Chef Daniel for the evening, paired with the right wine to go with every course.

Anne was impressed with the whole presentation, as she had not been to any Michelin-star restaurants before. They truly enjoyed the delicious courses served. And when the last course of the special dessert was served, Freddie pulled out a small velvet box from his pocket, went down on one knee, opened the box and said,

"Anne my love, no words can describe um how I felt when you told me you few days ago that changed your mind about what I am about to do. I told you I loved you the moment I met you. But my love for you since then, has gone way…way deeper and stronger. I want to spend the rest of my life with you um… will you marry me?"

Anne was utterly surprised and mesmerized seeing her Fredric on his knee proposing to her. Her misty eyes led to a pool of tears and conspicuous sobbing. Then, with a clear loud voice she said,

"Yes…yes… and a thousand times yes". Freddie stood up and put the huge diamond ring on her finger, hugged and kissed her with passion. The other guests in the restaurant applauded them cheerfully.

It took Anne a couple of minutes to settle down. She exchanged looks at Freddie and at her gorgeous ring, and started sobbing softly again. He held her hand and gave her a glass of champagne to help her relax. Then she asked him,

"Where did you get this amazing ring, it is incredibly beautiful?"

"I took you seriously when were talking last Saturday night after the wedding, when I pretended to be suspicious just to gain some time. But, inwardly I was so thrilled to hear you say you were amenable to marry me. So, on Monday I went straight to Harry Winston and ordered this solitaire for you." Freddie said gleefully.

"I'm so happy you took me seriously… How did you know my finger's size by the way?" Anne asked curiously.

"I stole one of your rings from the jewelry box."

"You, slick thief, you… I adore you, and I promise you my full loyalty and everlasting love." Anne said while drying her tears that kept falling down her cheeks.

They continued with few bites of the delicious dessert, and drank the champagne with a joyful heart, and an elevated mind. The commitment to one another was now cast in stone, and the fears of the past were demolished. Their eagerness to a happy future got printed boldly on their foreheads.

At home they gazed at one another in awe of what just happened. It became a celebration of a new beginning shrined with hope, faith and love. They remained silent for a while, smiling and devouring these precious moments and acknowledgment of what good life is all about. They pondered how they came a long way on their journey, from a past clouded with confusion and despair, from a state of misunderstanding to a present life of enlightenment joy and wisdom.

Then they broke their silence, and expressed their true love for one another, by continuing the celebration of the night with a mystical embrace that transcended into objectified sensual feelings, the like of which, they never experienced before.

***

After an unforgettable evening Saturday night, they woke up finding themselves in each other's arms and their bodies intertwined as one. Freddie smiled at Anne and she responded with a warm kiss and a pleasant "good morning". They took their time before they stepped out from the bed, looking forward to a newly born day with true happiness and peace of mind.

They were in such a joyful peace of mind and while Anne was preparing fresh coffee and toast, Freddie loaded the CD of Placido Domingo singing loudly the great aria 'Nessum Dorma' from the opera Turandot by Puccini. He attempted to join the great tenor in raising his pitch to the final expression of victory, 'I Vincero'. Anne was dumbfounded seeing him dance around and singing, she couldn't stop but giggle and say,

"Wow! You are an opera singer too! What other hidden talents have you been blessed with my love?" Anne asked.

"I am celebrating the victory of our engagement in my unique style of expression. I already won, my dear, I won… I didn't have to wait any longer!" Freddie confirmed.

When he sat down to enjoy his coffee with Anne, he said,

"I am so blessed dear Anne! 'I was truly lost and I am found' as Barry kept telling me lately… I—I rejoice by the transformation I recently went through, and thanks to your motivating advice too… I feel fresh again, and the past is—is totally forgotten. I want you to know that I feel exceptionally energized by our pledge of last night. I see us having um… a great future together on all fronts: emotionally, mentally, physically and spiritually. It is our spiritual intent to help others that will further enhance and invigorate the other aspects of our lives… I congratulate you for your wisdom to share this vision with me and I thank you for your devoted love too."

"I completely understand your feelings and the blessings that have been bestowed upon us… Six months ago, I wouldn't have even dreamt of the life I am living now with you. I—I feel so exceptionally rewarded and I'm totally grateful for where I am at today… The job you trusted me with, the love you have demonstrated and your sincere desire to help others, are all rare qualities that I am privileged to enjoy sharing, with a man of your rare caliber." Anne responded.

The newly engaged couple agreed to have a light lunch around the corner and then take a relaxed Sunday walk in Central Park, their favorite landmark of good memories.

***

I came back from our honeymoon Sunday evening and the first call I made was to my buddy Freddie. After sharing with him the highlights of the week we enjoyed in Hawaii he told me that he got engaged to Anne. I almost dropped the phone when I heard that and I said,

"What? Did I hear you well? Did you say engaged, as in proposing to marry her?"

"Yes, all the above!" I replied

"When? How? Why without me knowing about it?" I asked.

"Yesterday, I knelt and proposed in a restaurant. I don't need to tell you why I proposed, you thick-headed friend, because it is all your fault." Freddie teased.

"My fault? How is that?" I wanted to know.

"It's your wedding event that wetted our appetite and paved the way. While talking with her after your ceremony I found out she was amenable to the concept of another, despite her big disappointment the first time. You softened the pad you rascal, and I seized the occasion to take immediate action." Freddie said proudly.

"Congratulations! I'm thrilled to hear this news… Melody, come here…" I called Melody in the other room to tell her the good news.

"Say hi, and let's get together soon!" Freddie said before he hung up the phone.

Anne informed Lara and her parents, while Freddie called his Mother and they were all excited about the engagement news.

***

The office saw Anne walk in on Monday morning, with a happy smile on her face, and Melody was the first to see her. She hugged and congratulated her in the presence of all the others who jumped in to do the same and to see the gorgeous ring on her finger. Anne was elated to see this warm reception and seized the opportunity to tell them that she would like to have an evaluation meeting in the conference room in one hour.

The staff gathered around the conference table and Anne asked them for their opinion of the work so far and what new ideas do they recommend to add. Vera, the vice president said her team, with the help of Melody also, are quiet busy handling the various emails and inquiries that keep coming by phone, or in writing. She added that she would like to send out two members of her team to visit with important contacts that called for further clarifications before they commit to a donation. Anne told her to do it.

The accountant stated they have a total of $2.9 M in the account after the first month expenses including the grand opening. He told Anne that he estimates the monthly expenses to be close to $180,000, or about $2.1 M a year. He recommended an accelerated rate to raise funds, to maintain a healthy reserve in the account at all times.

Anne listened to other remarks and then said,

"We need to keep the momentum going and focus on smaller donations that are pledged monthly or quarterly, in addition to the generous one time donations we received. So please reach out to more individuals, to donate small amounts. It is the multitude of them that counts. Vera, you are an expert in this field and I depend on you to beef up this new program. I personally will donate all the fees I receive from my private practice to DAA. Besides, it is tax deductible. Fredric takes good care of me, and DAA is my priority now.

"I am also recruiting the women I treat to become fundraisers themselves. They are willing to scout the field and refer us to new circles of society. Currently I help a total of 18 patients on a weekly basis or an average of 3 a day. I expect this number to double soon if I don't control it. I will limit the number to 24 patients a week in order to leave ample time for the affairs of DAA. As we grow bigger, I will reduce the number of patients on a decrescendo basis.

"Please do not hesitate to discuss anything you have in your mind. My door is always open. Thank you and have a wonderful day!"

Anne and her employees worked diligently, and their joint achievements together as a team were remarkable. Freddie visited DAA offices a couple times a week, and his presence was always received with gratitude and appreciation by all the staff.

Meanwhile, Melody and I moved to the new apartment and our relationship with Freddie and Anne, our new neighbors, was further enhanced by closer attention and care to one another. Our honeymoon in Hawaii a year ago was productive and Melody gave birth to a lovely baby boy nine months later. Without any hesitation we called him Fredric. Mr. 'Sensitivo', as I called my buddy once, was touched by our pregnancy, and was prompted to discuss and agree with adorable Anne on a wedding date.

Freddie and Anne decided to get married on the second Saturday of September that year, and had a very stupendous idea about their wedding plans. They decided to have a private civil wedding at city hall in New York, and the ceremony to follow a week later, at the famous Medici villa just outside Florence, in Tuscany Italy. Anne asked Lara to be her maid of honor, and I, of course, was the best man.

The arrangement was perfect for what they had in mind. The invitation was for 30 people only, mostly close friends and family. Freddie reserved the main villa and its adjacent 5 other villas for three nights with accommodations for up to 32 guests. Both had visited Florence in mid August and selected this venue after checking out few others. This cozy place suited their plans perfectly. He offered free air tickets to all the guests flying from the United States and room and board was also provided for free.

Among his guests, Freddie invited his mother, Matilda and her Doctor friend John, his two sons, his two mangers and their wives, Laura and her husband, and James and his wife. Anne invited her parents, her aunt and uncle, Lara and her fiancé, and Vera and her husband, her private secretary and her husband.

The occasion was magnificently executed and it was one of the most elegant and classy weddings any one could have. Every thing went very smoothly and the guests were grateful, had a lot of fun in Florence and felt honored to take part in the ceremony.

The newly weds took another week off after the wedding and drove around the southern part of Italy starting in Rome, to Napoli, and to Positano on the Amalfi coast. They spent a wonderful time on their honeymoon and were warmly received, by their staff when they returned back home to New York.

Epilogue

The reputation of Fredric Rodman and Anne Stevenson Rodman grew to higher levels in the ensuing years that followed. Their personal relationship became a fine example for many couples to emulate. They did not brag about their success, be it in his real estate business for Fredric, or the respectable reputation and successful achievements of DAA led by Anne. Their humility attracted more people to sponsor and donate money and support to their mission.

In the first year of DAA's operation a total of 4300 women and 300 men subscribed to their magazine. Eighty percent of the subscribers also registered as regular donors, albeit for quarterly amounts ranging from $50 to $100 each. The first year generated an income of $1,380,000 from these individual donors. The VIP donors from large corporations and banks added an additional $2.2 million to DAA's account.

Before the end first year, Anne could only have time to treat 20 women privately and she contributed all her earnings to DAA, which amounted to more than $120,000. As such, she had time to manage DAA as the CEO, and she gave 6 lectures to different women groups and conferences. Anne also recruited a total of 32 women who volunteered to spend at least two hours a day to help other women in need within their relevant communities.

Additionally, 24 women attended DAA classes and learned new skills that took them away from the non-dignified work they did before. There were 7 cases of women abused by men that DAA succeeded to refer to the police, and had these men reprimanded or punished by the judges in their communities.

The judge released Jane form prison on probation, after eight months. She worked diligently for DAA under the supervision of Vera. She did a good job convincing several women to abstain from doing what she had done before. A good many of the women she helped ended up taking classes at DAA and learned new skills and found good jobs that equipped them to live a decent life.

Jane respected Anne the boss, and thanked Freddie for her early release from Jail. She pledged her dedication to help DAA as much as she could. She kept a formal relationship with either one of them.

Anne continued to expand the mission of DAA in the years that followed and succeeded to open new chapters in five other major cities in the country. And before the end of the third year Anne delivered a beautiful baby girl they called Lisa.

Fredric Rodman and I, best friends since we were 18, our freshman year in college. I observed a unique journey about personal growth and transformation. Up until recently, Freddie used to refer to me as his alter ego. He was a brilliant, but troubled, young man, unloved as a child, yet spoiled with external abundance. He was often angry and confused about his life priorities.

He then reached a crossroad in his midlife where he didn't know which direction to take. Wisely, he chose the road less travelled and went through an intensive period of inner search and self-realization to end his suffering and loss of focus. He discovered that his search for true love had to start by practicing self-love first. That was the turning point in his life for the better.

Fredric now lives a life fulfilled with purpose, and energized by inner joy and dedication to help others. He must have been also heavenly guided, when he met Anne. This special woman encouraged him to follow a new path, and graciously agreed to become his wife. They are both on the same journey to reach out and help others. Their success story continued to blossom in the years that followed with positive influence on many people. I know their story influenced my own life.

After many long years, I am no longer Fredric Rodman's *alter ego* and, he doesn't wake me up drunk after midnight anymore. He has become my *idol*.

Love Is All There Is.

CPSIA information can be obtained
at www.ICGtesting.com
Printed in the USA
BVHW031718230621
610293BV00002B/147